dyke london

GW00367849

a guide

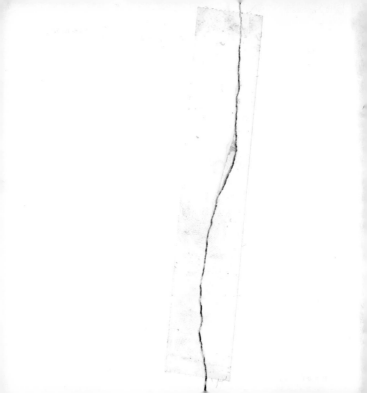

rosa ainley

photographs by heike löwenstein

dyke london

a guide

● ● ● ellipsis

•••

BRITISH LIBRARY CATALOGUING IN PUBLICATION
A CIP record for this book is available from the British Library

PUBLISHED BY •••ellipsis
2 Rufus Street London N1 6PE
www http://www.ellipsis.com
SERIES EDITOR Tom Neville
SERIES DESIGN Jonathan Moberly
EDITOR Vicky Wilson

COPYRIGHT © 2001 Ellipsis London Limited

ISBN 1 84166 054 X

PRINTING AND BINDING Hong Kong

•••ellipsis is a trademark of Ellipsis
London Limited

For a copy of the Ellipsis catalogue or
information on special quantity orders
of Ellipsis books please contact
the sales department on
020–7739 3157 or sales@ellipsis.co.uk

dyke london: a guide

Rosa Ainley 2000

contents

Introduction

Between them, two openings and two closures (of the many) since the first edition of *dyke london* express neatly the story of what's happening in lesbian London. The Ace of Clubs, the city's longest-running club at more than 20 years – always full although rarely would anyone you knew admit to having been there – finally closed. An institution grudgingly admired for its longevity, the Ace was never solely the tourist haunt that many London residents claimed, but it was always there and easy to find in Piccadilly. Rumours in the City now supplies more of the same, on a larger scale (see page 5.36). Islington's Angel Bar – known as the 'Fallen Angel' and site of big stand-offs between pro- and anti-SM dykes in the mid 1980s – was one of London's first modern gay bars. As its popularity faded it became known more recently as the 'Well of Loneliness'. At the time it caught the spirit of a new mixed gay scene, until then much more gender-segregated, which has its legacy in the present where most 'lesbian' venues in the capital actually admit the species known as 'men as guests'.

All this history – sex wars at the Fallen Angel, straight dykes at the Ace of Clubs – seems quite ancient now, and the two openings underline that. The lesbian scene in London now straddles a strip club in Soho and a salon in SoTo – that's South Tottenham to you and me. So – between slipping dollar bills into the garter of a pole dancer at Loose (see page 5.28) and enjoying the artistic and literary ambience of Tart (see page 2.16) – are we all catered for?

Around half the entries in this second edition of *dyke london* are either completely new or updated, which, in just over a year, bespeaks a fluid situation. High turnover is a common complaint about the scene, but turnover isn't necessarily such a drawback. Places rise and fall with the tides of popularity; freshness can be as great an attraction as the known and cherished. It isn't only lesbian and gay clubs that have become move-able feasts, changing to suit new venues and conditions.

Despite the widespread opinion that the lesbian scene has very little to offer, there is a huge assortment of activities prefaced with the L-word. *dyke london* doesn't attempt to cover every lesbian or les/gay activity; it is impossible to include the network of special-interest and discussion groups; the array of services from electricians to therapists to vets; or the army of complementary-medicine practitioners (see Media, page 0.4).

dyke london is a selective guide, bringing you the best, the worst and some of the bizarre happenings that come under the lesbian leisure heading. It gives a critical appraisal of what's happening rather than 'what's on'; it should be equally of interest – though for different reasons – to residents and visitors; those new to the London scene, whether due to sexuality or geography, and those who have been partaking of it for years. Not to mention those who have a passing interest.

And that may be a lot of women. *The New Hite Report* revealed that 71 per cent of women would like to 'try' a same-sex relationship (which makes it sound like a new brand of toothpaste); its publication overlapped with a flurry of faux coming-out tales in the press. Yes, sexual tourism or testing out the lesbian sexual option has (yet again) had plenty of columns devoted to it in the press. Whether this will have any effect on the lesbian scene, or whether it's merely another fad to spice up boring sex lives and boring pages, a manifestation of ladette behaviour, remains to be seen. It's probably just boring old titillation for the lads but it's likely that for some women who are genuinely questioning their sexuality it will operate as a cover.

But before we leap gratefully to the conclusion that the climate in London and beyond is growing more tolerant of the queer persuasion,

dyke london: a guide

there have also been dangerous and depressing indications to the contrary, most seriously the bomb in Soho's Old Compton Street in April 1999 (see page 1.2). From Stoke Newington, with undoubtedly one of London's highest lesbian populations, there have been reports of harassment leading to the closure of two venues in the first six months of 2000. And nationwide, the campaign to repeal Section 28, the pernicious legislation that prohibits the 'promotion of homosexuality as an acceptable family relationship' has brought forth all sorts of homophobic lowlife bleating, in a thoroughly uninformed fashion, about 'protecting the children'. Well, what about our children? Despite preaching tolerance and inclusiveness, the current government looks unlikely to strike Section 28 from the books, or will replace it with equally reactionary legislation.

Other innovations aside from Loose and Tart include The Observatory Film Club, a non-profit-making women-only club for low- and zero-budget film screenings. Worth looking out for in the future, though gone to ground at time of writing, is ModFarm, a soul club/art collective. Their events became, after a sojourn in Clerkenwell, only trackable on the internet and then disappeared, hopefully only temporarily. Another event definitely worth mentioning though outside of the scope of this book (new section: couch potatoes?) is *Rhona*, the new lesbian sit com, starring and co-written by comedian Rhona Cameron of *Gaytime* TV fame. We've had lesbians on TV; we've had Dyke TV (transmitted very late on Saturday nights), but this was a definite first and one which needed stabilisers to cope with the full force of mass lesbian opinion, quite apart from the reaction from the general public.

Possibly the opposite of innovation, the festival formerly known as Pride or even, whisper it, Lesbian and Gay Pride, has now been renamed as cuddly Mardi Gras. Gays just wanna have carnival, apparently. But although a name speaks volumes, whatever it's called the shouting never stops and Mardi Gras is still mired in controversy (see page 2.12).

It's noticeable that 'disco' has crept back into the lexicon, part of the unsatiable appetite for 1970s trash nights and camping it up on the dance-floor. Disco also, in different contexts, operates as code for easy, friendly nights for people uninterested in uptown cooler-than-thou clubs.

Niches seem to be where it's at then – unsurprisingly, if you consider that it's lesbians from teenagers to women well beyond pension age who feature in these pages, and very occasionally on the same page (see Fried Green Tomatoes, page 8.6, and Loose, page 5.28). Everyone needs some-where to go, and often someone exists to provide it. A 'let's make our own, then' attitude has lead to several events like The Observatory Film Club and Vita's (see pages 2.8 and 5.46), both independent, non-profit affairs. But the high-profile career entrepreneurs such as Amy Lamé, Kim Lucas, Charlotte Harris and Valerie Mason-John continue to offer what she wants too.

And because we don't only come out at night to frequent seedy bars, *dyke london* includes much more than bars and clubs – places not usually considered to be part of the lesbian itinerary such as the National Portrait Gallery and the Chelsea Physic garden. So *dyke london* covers places that may be of interest to you whether or not your social life is defined by your sexuality, and whether your preferences run to women-only, les/gay venues and events, or places where sexuality is recognised but immaterial.

dyke london: a guide

Media

You're as likely to find *Marie Claire*, *Elle Deco* or *Sleaze Nation* in a dyke's magazine rack, but if you want lesbian/gay publications this is the range you can choose from. Most of them also have websites so you can check them out on-line before you buy.If your local newsagent can't oblige, you can try WHSmith – with new-found tolerance they stock *Diva* and *Attitude* (a kind of *Arena* for gay men) in some branches and have promised to stock *Fluid*. The US publications listed can usually be found in gay bookshops (see page 9.2).

Diva The UK's first and only national lesbian magazine, *Diva* covers all aspects of lesbian life and style including news, travel, parenting, music, horoscopes and problem page, as well as extensive listings and mail-order books. *Diva* launched a fiction imprint in May 2000. Monthly, £2. www.gaytimes.com

Outcast First published in 1999, *Outcast* (strapline: 'The gay magazine that dares to be different') is an independent magazine supplying the news the 'gay media mafia' shies away from. Monthly, £2. www.outcastmagazine.co.uk

Gay Times From the Millivres stable (as is *Diva*), *Gay Times* is mainly for men but does have some lesbian coverage, usually in the book- and film-review sections. Monthly, £2.95. www.gaytimes.com

Fluid Launched in April 2000, *Fluid* is the first production from Chronos (who also produce the *Pink Paper*) that you have to pay for. Billed as a lifestyle magazine – this is strictly for the boyz, unless of course you really want to read about Dale Winton giving up fags. Monthly, £2.50.

Curve One of the first glossies for lesbians, *Curve* was originally called Deneuve until the Catherine in question threatened legal action. A stylish and entertaining affair, covering lesbian-related news, politics, pop culture, lots of celeb features and gossip, etc. Eight issues annually, £3.50. www.curvemag.com

Girlfriends With in-depth features and regular columns including Pat Califia, author of many books on lesbian sexuality and porn, as agony aunt, Girlfriends covers culture and politics from a lesbian perspective. Monthly, £3.75

www.girlfriendsmag.com

On Our Backs is a lesbian sex mag first published in the US in the 1980s. Mainly erotic photography and fiction, it also covers lesbian cultural stuff. Bi-monthly, £4.50.

www.onourbacksmag.com

Free papers are available in all gay bars and clubs and in many mainstream bookshops.

Pink Paper A free weekly tabloid distributed nationally, with news, features, listings, and acres of personals. Pretty thin, much mocked, but someone's got to do it.

www.sonow.net

Axiom Another free weekly tabloid distributed nationally, with more news than the *Pink*, and, dramatically, no TV listings.

Boyz Enough said really: useful for TV/listings if there's really nothing else.

WEBSITES

It was only in 1999 that the UK got its first interactive lesbian website, which was the *Pink Paper*-stable mate dykesnow. Due to apathy or lack of time or money, there hasn't been a huge rush of lesbian internet activity. But now that everyone and her cat – and there will probably be a site for her soon too, if there isn't already – are on-line, the internet scene for dykes could be starting to change. While a lot of content may be on a straightforward listings and lifestylee level, and fairly forgettable, access to the internet could be an important method of contact for isolated, new or housebound lesbians. At the moment many sites are more or less replicating the publications to which they are attached, a missed opportunity and a situation that will probably change as more people explore the possibilities of the medium.

A good place to start for new users could be to go to one of the lesbian or gay magazine sites, the site of your favourite club, some of which now have their own web pages (and hopefully more up-to-date listings than the press), or one of those listed below. You can then go wherever the links or your fancy takes you. Mardi Gras and the film festival (see pages 2.12 and 2.2) have sites too; these are useful for updates on what's happening and for booking tickets.

dykesnow Set up by the publishers of the *Pink Paper*, who also offer SoNow, a free internet service provider (calls charged at national rate) dykesnow is the 'first dyke-only website in the UK made by gay women for gay women and not simply tagged on to the end of a gay boy site'.

As the name suggests it covers more than the lesbian sections of the *Pink Paper* – listings, personals, interviews, reviews, links to interior design, clubs, travel, fashion sites and chat rooms. Users can set up their own home pages, or join in forum discussions (simple instructions provided), secure in the knowledge that strict security checks mean men trying to join up are weeded out. Also worth checking out is Dyke Galleries, pictures of women who answered an ad in the paper for images of 'real' lesbians – if your tastes run more to the unreal, any of the straight porn sites will sort you out. Most interesting is the piece on webcam sites, exploring all the voyeuristic possibilities, and all so affordable for an outlay of only £70. dykesnow was due to be relaunched in July 2000.

www.rainbownetwork.com Some lesbian content here and you can sign up to have les/gay news updates e-mailed to you – useful in theory but often the links aren't up. Recently had a feature, 'Everything you wanted to ask about lesbians but were afraid to ask', which seemed a strange choice seeing that most site visitors would know the answers already, unless they're going for the sexual-tourist vote, or perhaps it has something to do with rainbownetwork's listing in *The Guardian*'s *Editor* magazine 'sites to watch' page as 'of largely gay interest'.

To the question, 'What the hell is butch and femme?' the answer was that butch and femme was invented in the 1950s to imitate straights, which might lead you to doubt the accuracy of other site content … and anyway, the first question should be, 'So what do you do in bed?'

www.outcastmagazine.com The *Outcast* magazine site, and of interest to anyone who doesn't subscribe to the mainstream gay 'party line' as broadcast by most of the gay media (*Outcast* calls it the gay mafia). The site was taken down after a libel suit threat from the *Pink Paper* but is now operative again. Very good on links including UK and worldwide sites (find out what's happening in Zimbabwe and Iran), community and campaigning sites, newsgroups.

queerlondon To be relaunched in July 2000. Its previous incarnation most enjoyably and ludicrously featured tours around town with several lesbians and gay men, telling you their favourite clubs, restaurants, etc. Basically you picked whoever you figured would be most taste-compatible with you and clicked. Otherwise fairly standard.

planetout.com Links with the US magazine *Advocate*, planetout features news bulletins, travel jobs, romance and dating, 'tips for new moms' (now there's a market left untapped), a daily poll and features on queer television. It isn't especially scintillating, but the news coverage is quite interesting if you want to know what Americans hear about what's going on in the US.

www.lesbian.org/lesbian-lists The sheer diversity of the lists of chat sites here make this worth a visit or two. International and fascinatingly comprehensive.

www.lesbian.com With links from land dykes and spirituality to business and economy, lesbian.com is a favourite. How can you resist the 'Museum of Menstruation' and 'How to pee standing up'?

www.damron.com Worldwide dyke travel site, with a strong US perspective, selling holidays and flights and Damron guides. Lots of information there; you have to subscribe to get any details but I can tell you that it lists 68 gay bars in London.

www.whatsonwhere.com This is a worldwide 'what's on' site with lesbian and gay section among its offerings. It's in the process of being built up, but major cities/events are already up. Useful to look up details about anywhere you're travelling to.

streets

Old Compton Street

Often referred to as Queer Street or Boystown – venues for lesbians being in short supply here, though not lesbians themselves – this is the central strip of Soho, and a testament to the power of the pink pound and the 1980s commercialisation of the scene: 'we're here, we're queer and we're going shopping'. Superficial Old Compton Street may be, but the nail-bomb explosion in the Admiral Duncan (following those in Brixton and Brick Lane in the two preceding weeks) in April 1999, which killed three people, served as a strong corrective to anyone who imagined that fear of bigotry only existed in the imaginations of the paranoid and fanatic. Old Compton Street is a fluffy paradise only for the few, but having one street in London where you can safely kiss your girl-/boyfriend in public is apparently too much for some. We're here, we're queer: get used to it.

Whatever your attitude to it – and for many Old Compton Street represents the worst of gay chauvinism and shallowness – there are plenty of places worth visiting in the area. You can do some heavy-duty gay shopping in American Retro or Clone Zone, invest in your own speculum at Paradise bodyworks, or, if like me you're more interested in your stomach than your cervix, invest very heavily in Fratelli Camisa – the only Italian deli left in the street – and then sit in one of many cafés, bars and restaurants in the street. In each case you can choose gay-dedicated venues or not.

Freedom bar and café, allegedly once owned by George Michael, just around the corner in Wardour Street, is no longer as paralysingly trendy as it once was. It's much more of a gay/straight mix than it used to be, so you may want to make a point of going in to keep a reasonable level of queerness, or avoid it. It can be very pleasant in summer when the wall of glazing facing the street is opened, and it looks particularly pretty in the early evening when the coloured sculptural lighting comes into its

own. Newer on the block and with its gay credentials intact is Manto Soho (the 'Soho' is just in case you got confused and thought you were in Manchester, where Manto was the first 'new' gay bar to grace Canal Street). Old Compton Street Café, full of identikit Billy-boys, is open 24 hours for coffees and snacks, as is Bar Italia, with outside seating *de rigeur* even in winter, the perfect vantage point from which to view the street. It also boasts a widescreen TV: avoid during football matches unless you're a fan. Comptons is not an option for women, but you may like to know that Wagner wrote part of the Ring Cycle in a building on the same site.

Amato's *pasticceria* is less famous and so less crowded than Valerie's, and even if the cakes are, an undercover Italian cake-maker confided, not authentic, the waitresses are lesbian-friendly. You share tables and get to hear other people's conversations and you can sit for hours over a coffee and a plate of cinnamon toast if the Italian pop music doesn't get to you first.

For more serious eating, there's Balans (see page 8.2) for modern gay lifestyle; Presto's, famous for being the late Derek Jarman's favourite restaurant and for its waitresses; Little Italy, the sister establishment to Bar Italia; Satsuma in Wardour Street for noodles; Mildred's in Greek Street for vegetarian food with a less frenetic Soho feel; and about a million other places. Its faults may be legion, but Old Compton Street is not short on food.

ADDRESS Old Compton Street, London WC2
UNDERGROUND Tottenham Court Road/Leicester Square

Stoke Newington Church Street

Multiple opportunities for heavy eye-contact exist in Church Street – in restaurants, cafés, pubs, shops, cemetery and the park. Indeed, if lesbians went in for cruising seriously, this could be the strip. It may come as something of a surprise then that Church Street itself boasts neither lesbian bar nor club. But you don't have to go far to find one. Both Due South and Blush are five minutes away (see pages 4.14 and 4.6), The Oak Bar (see page 4.26) is close by in Newington Green, and DJ and quiz*meister* Viv Acious runs Route 73, a weekly vinyl-fest in the nearby Londesborough pub, at 36 Barbauld Road.

At the High Street end it's a battle between estate agents and restaurants, enlivened by occasional eccentricities such as Rosa's lingerie shop (mind the dog) and the Irish Women's Centre. A poster is on sale of Stoke Newington shopfronts, which sums up what Church Street is about; Brighton has one, and doubtless other so-called middle-youth locations do too. Further along towards Clissold Park is a violin shop, an upmarket video shop, two alternative health centres, three second-hand bookshops, Joanne's Plantique (prize-winning name, if not flowers) and Abney Park cemetery – a great attraction and a popular cruising ground for gay men. Finally you come to the curved splendour of the municipal offices (built in 1937) where lesbian events such as the popular Christmas-time Emma Peel Fanclub, local happenings and wedding receptions are held.

Church Street is a place of much pavement seating and many cafés, including the Clissold Park café with prized tables looking out over the park, The Cooler with its café space behind the delicatessen, and The Blue Legume, specialising in coffees, juice combos and fiendishly healthy drinks such as wheatgrass. Or there's the Vortex, which in the evenings becomes a jazz club, often featuring well-known lesbian artistes. During the day it has a slightly moleish air – as if it had woken up too early and

streets

was unaccustomed to daylight – but it's cheaper and less full of itself than many of Church Street's alternatives.

There are too many restaurants to mention – you certainly won't go hungry. Particularly recommended are Rasa for south-Indian vegetarian and Mesclun for modern European.

Beyond the shops is Clissold Park and Clissold House, built in the 1790s, with the café on one side, formal rosbeds to the other. Other attractions include a small aviary, a herd of goats, deer, a paddling pool, and a lake. Several lesbian football and softball teams (see page 10.20) have been known to practise here – if you rounded up all the dykes you saw between the beginning of Church Street and the park on any Saturday you could probably make up an entire Premier League division.

ADDRESS Stoke Newington Church Street, London N16
BUS 67, 73, 106, 149, 243

events

Lesbian and Gay Film Festival

An undisputed highlight in the capital's lesbian and gay calendar, the festival offers a ten-day preening opportunity at a South Bank brimming over with queerness, ideally timetabled for spring, when the sap is rising. And there are films too, features, documentaries and shorts, premieres and revivals, panel discussions and special club nights, featuring work by established and unknown film-makers from across the globe.

But if the films become almost immaterial for some people in the face of this social whirl, the festival gets more impressive each year. In 1999 the festival smash was the much-imitated *Singalonga Sound of Music*; *Cine-oke* was the 2000 model set to repeat its success.

Isaac Julien and Mira Nair showcased new work at the festival in 2000. You could also catch films featuring Gena Rowlands, Mariel Hemingway, Tyne Daly, Sara Gilbert (Darlene from *Rosesanne*) and Susannah York. Opening- and closing-night gala screenings in the West End have become like court functions: as much 'must be there' as 'must see'.

You can make a day – or indeed a ten-dayer – of it by watching a film in the afternoon, then settling in for tea, cake and crowd-watching in the NFT café. In good weather you can watch the les/gay riverside promenade. Then before your evening film, wander down to The Cut – past the IMAX cinema – where plenty of food can be found, at Live Bait (see page 8.8) if you're feeling rich, Konditor and Cook in the Young Vic if you're not, or Dom Felipe, where you can order tapas to suit your wallet.

ADDRESS National Film Theatre, South Bank, London SE1
(020 7928 3232) www.llgff.org.uk
OPEN two weeks during March/April
ACCESS call box office for programme details and ticket prices
UNDERGROUND Waterloo

Drag King and Queen/Lesbian Beauty Contest

The Drag King and Queen and Lesbian Beauty Contest have become fixtures in the lesbian calendar, on alternate years; and that's not all. There are now two rival outfits both promoting beauty contests, headed by Amy Lamé (see page 5.8), who organised the original, and Valerie Mason-John. It's a moot point whether London is big enough for two beauty contests and feelings will probably run high.

In 1999 20 drag kings and queens of various persuasions were up for the crown. The drag kings, possibly of greater interest to most dykes, approximated a wide range of aspects of masculinity with lots of stick-on facial hair, teamed with mini-skirts, kilts, classy/tarty French-pleat hairdos, as well as the expected uniforms (George Michael/George the Policeman, Leatherman Sam). But some contestants didn't make much effort at all and looked just generally butch, and so fervently do they embrace certain trappings of manhood that they looked like the kind of men who inspire jokes about small dicks. Memorable drag queens were Morticia and Clare Tramp-disco slut.

It's a very mix-and-match evening, as is the stage, decorated with suggestions of gold braid, combat netting, pink tulle, to cover all bases. In a neat touch the emcees, Queenie and Jean T, swap their queen/king outfits for the second half. If not all versatility of gender is here, you can marvel at least at the power of performance.

In previous years judges have included Sam Fox, newly bisexual and no longer born again; in 1999 we had Daniella Nardini (Anna from *This Life*), looking ever-so-slightly embarrassed and wearing Birkies as a sop to the audience; Jackie Clune; and Miss Kimberley, drag queen about town. There's a couple of recognisable celebrities, including Hayley-the-transsexual from *Coronation Street*, and someone who turns out to be

Drag King and Queen/Lesbian Beauty Contest

Drag King and Queen/Lesbian Beauty Contest

Daniella Nardini's mum sitting at the white-clothed tables at the front of the stage. Champagne in buckets raises the tone a little, but it's mostly tins of Red Stripe for the rest of us. The winner was a dead cert: Vincent P Zazz, continuing something of a jazz tradition, who sang 'Just a bad case of opposite sex' with his band.

Queens and Kings look good on the publicity but do they really go together? Bit of a mismatch there, perhaps, but what they do all have in common is more front than Selfridges and this is a night for suspension of disbelief and cynicism, certainly not one for philosophical deliberation on gender.

ADDRESS check press for details
MIX gay and straight
ACCESS check press for details

Drag King and Queen/Lesbian Beauty Contest

The Observatory

Are you a practicing homosexual?
Actually I'm a little out of practice.
From *Disgraceful Conduct*, directed by Eva Weber

Dykes into independent films and those who like the hit-and-miss of the shorts at the Lesbian and Gay Film Festival (see page 2.2) can now get their kicks on a monthly basis. The Observatory exists to promote women film and video makers and give a showcase to zero- and low-budget films in the congenial surroundings of the Ritzy Cinema and café. Recognising that without connections in the industry film makers have little opportunity to show their work, three women have set up this non-profit organisation in their spare time.

Upstairs at the Ritzy café (also home to the Sewing Circle bar, another dyke-friendly Brixton event) it's like watching films in a private screening room, and there's the unaccustomed pleasure of smoking at the cinema. One end of the room has a glass wall and balcony with tables and chairs which could be a good spot in the summer; at the other is the screen on a mirrored wall, so the space doesn't seem so small. At the height of London mayoral fever, I couldn't help noticing that some of the chairs were stamped with the GLC Women's Committee symbol, lending the whole affair a sense of history. Music and a Bollywood film played as a backdrop while we waited for the six short films. One of the writers was on hand to chat to anyone who wanted to ask questions, and an invitation was made to anyone who has a film to screen.

The café itself, multi-levelled with an aluminium bar, has table football, snacks and a good beer selection, and it's a groovy Ritzy crowd who turn up. The Observatory isn't just a local night, it's worth travelling for and plenty of women turn up alone. Films here aren't going to be to everyone's

taste: not recommended for Hollywood addicts or preview and Carlton advertisement junkies. But it's a welcome and inspired addition to the scene as well as an on-going alternative to the festival, with themed nights in the offing, and possibly a move to a larger space which already looks like it might be needed.

ADDRESS The Ritzy Cinema/Café, Coldharbour Lane, London sw2; 07931 461022 (Observatory number)/020 7837 0188 (Sundays only)
e-mail avie@observatory9971.freeserve.co.uk
OPEN approximately every six weeks, call for details
ACCESS £3, membership
MIX women-only
UNDERGROUND Brixton

Pride/Mardi Gras

For some lesbians and gays Pride is like Christmas (as in 'Happy Pride'), only without the horror of going 'home' to the 'family'. But nuclear night-mares aside, there are other takes on Christmas: for many people it's something that's lots of fun the first few times but difficult to get excited about year after year. Take your corners everybody please.

Whatever your feelings about it, there's no doubt that every year Pride involves some element of community crisis. In 1999 the crisis turned out to be only a rumour: that the local council was going to cut off the power after 20.00 following complaints from residents, and leave us with Pride Unplugged, a not entirely unpleasing idea to some, but disturbingly early 1990s. But at least it happened. In 1998 Pride, amid raging arguments in the gay press about the politics or lack of them and the name and its in/exclusiveness, became for the first time a ticketed rather than a free event, and was then cancelled, due to various financial difficulties, a fiasco that ensured the bad press will run and run. Pride™ – it had finally come to this. Little space left for the politics/celebration debate, then. The change of name to Mardi Gras in 1999, contentious in itself, has done nothing to leave this past behind.

For some people, the march through central London on a Saturday afternoon – with floats, disco beats, drag queens, bizarre banners for esoteric groups, drummers and the god-awful whistles – is an essential part of celebrating gay pride, making ourselves visible with tens of thousands of other queers. For others it's meaningless, old-fashioned, and eminently missable.

The choice of Finsbury Park for Mardi Gras in 1999 was definitely a winner on one count: that the not-very-mysterious closure of train stations which had always accompanied the post-march trek to the park since Pride began didn't happen. But something had to justify a £10 entry

(increased to £10/15, depending on where you bought your tickets in 2000). Would it be the inflated drink prices, the ban on people bringing their own food, the bar queues, the dodgy PAS (sorry, acts)? Room for big improvements was the general verdict.

At time of writing, allegations of mismanagement have already been levelled by the magazine *Outcast* (see page 0.4) against Mardi Gras 2000, the company organising the event, who dismissed them as 'clerical errors' and issued assurances that the event will go ahead, which fuel suspicion that it won't (it did). When the company says it will introduc spaces in the park for parents and children, people of colour, and people who like different kinds of music, you can't help thinking that a ticket entitles you to exactly what wasn't working in the first place, for free. Still, scepticism aside, there are signs of new departures for 2000 with a festival season at the ICA including comedian Donna McPhail and popular clubnights with Sister India and the Emma Peel Fanclub (see pages 1.6 and 5.26).

If you're still up for it after a march and a party, there's plenty of choice on the night. Like New Year's Eve, it's an opportunity for club promoters to organise special events, some overpriced and overfull to be sure, but usually some good one-off nights in addition to the usual Saturday-night fare. So choose carefully to extend your pleasure into the next day.

ADDRESS often the march begins at Hyde Park and ends close to Victoria; after the march, the party will (probably) be in a major park
www.londonmardigras.com
OPEN often first Saturday in July, 12.00–22.00; check press
MIX very
ACCESS probably by ticket from a gay outlet near you
UNDERGROUND Marble Arch/Hyde Park

Tart

Tart is a new phenomenon. It's a women's salon and gallery space in up-and-coming south Tottenham – SoTo to the cognoscenti – organised by Monika Bobinska (curator and ex-Meccano Club promoter) and host Reina Lewis (lecturer in cultural studies, fashion commentator and broadcaster). For me, a salon conjures up images of powdered wigs and courtesans *à la* Dame aux Camellias, or wildly creative types competing for attention round at Gertrude Stein and Alice B Toklas' house. Could be hard acts to follow, and I had been warned by one of the organisers that guests might not be arriving semi-naked by horse. Sadly, this proved to be the case but showery weather may have been to blame.

Aside from that disappointment, this gathering came through on all counts, with the intimacy of a houseparty, some people dressed (up) for the occasion, a poetry reading by Cherry Smyth and Barbara Norden and an exhibition by Breton artist Emmanuelle Vequeau providing a focus for the evening. Even though it may not be entirely in the spirit of the artistic/literary salons of the past, happily Tart doesn't take itself overly seriously: quizzes were distributed on the opening night and singles nights are among the events planned for the future along with performances, art shows, and readings. Naturally, tarts were served, along with toxic-coloured (but strangely delicious) fondant fancies.

Avoiding the possible pitfall of the evening turning into a seminar by keeping conversation going in small groups, there could be a danger that Tart would become a party with an art event attached, especially given the high level of previous acquaintance. But with a shifting attendance from event to event and with Reina Lewis on hand as the perfect hostess to make introductions as requested, this is sidestepped. Unlike most private views and launches where the work often takes second place to seeing who's there, at Tart the work on the walls (and in the garden) and

the poetry reading became a means for conversation.

People come to Tart either by invitation or by writing and saying why they'd like to attend. A space where people can display their work and have a response to it while socialising is an inspired idea, an enjoyable alternative to the usual round of the scene. Tart definitely has scarcity value. As somebody said, we all felt very grown up.

CONTACT www.tart-zone.com for invitation details
MIX women-only
ACCESS free (pay bar)

Summer Rites

Summer Rites has managed, in its first few years, to achieve a Pride-like gathering in a park with the usual attractions – beer, dancing, green space, a lucky bag of stage acts, club tents, a large number of lesbians and gays in the same place – and keep to a sensible size. The organisers call it an 'intimate party atmosphere' – maybe a slight exaggeration unless you have more than 60,000 friends – but in any case it's altogether more manageable than Pride. Summer Rites was originally conceived as a less sceney, less commercial Pride, but as the alternative inexorably becomes the mainstream it's now just another event, though one which avoids the censure to which Pride is prone. Financially, Summer Rites seems to have cracked it too: it was never free but paying £4 doesn't upset anyone, and anyway charging for Pride smacked of charging for Christmas, and each year various charities such as Rubberstuffers, the Eddie Surman Trust, Landmark and the Food Chain benefit from the event.

In sunny weather Summer Rites can be indeed be 'fun in the sun', a good place to hang out for the afternoon, dance a bit, drink a bit, shop even, just another summer festival. But it's considered to be 'more gay' than Mardi Gras which draws accusations of too many straight visitors from some quarters.

ADDRESS Brockwell Park, London SE24
OPEN usually first Saturday in August; check press for date and venue
MIX lesbian and gay
ACCESS ticket-only £4
BR Herne Hill
UNDERGROUND Brixton

pink plaques

Chelsea Girls

Though Hackney, one of the capital's poorest boroughs, has become the seat of London lesbianism – according to the 1980s dyke stereotype at least – there was a time when wealthy Chelsea was the place to be. This walk cuts a path to the doors of some famous, dead, upper-class lesbians.

It's a short bus ride from Sloane Square Underground down King's Road, just past Chelsea College where the chain stores peter out, to Bramerton Street, where 50 metres down on the left are the steps of Gateways, the infamous, solidly butch/femme, members-only club of the 1960s and 1970s. Lesbian folklore tells us it was an awful and wonderful place, where all classes mingled, even, among the large army contingent, officers and privates. It's astonishing now that Gateways could have existed in a street like this.

On the other side of King's Road is Carlyle Square, and at number 35 the gated, pillared home of Nancy Spain, founder with 'Jonnie' (Joan Werner Laurie) of *She* magazine. A semi-circle of landscaping at the pavement side and the residents-only garden in the square keep street noise and the public at bay. On the opposite side of the square is a plaque for Sir Oswald Sitwell (author and brother of Edith), but there is none for Nancy, who in the 1960s was practically the national lesbian treasure, appearing on *Juke Box Jury* in her impeccable hacking jackets.

Window-shop your way back down towards Sloane Square and turn right down Radnor Walk (towards Chelsea Embankment), then left into Redburn Street until you find Tite Street on the right. Oscar Wilde, who lived at number 34 between 1884 and 1894, has a Blue Plaque – one of three in a row – as a 'wit and dramatist'. None of the others is for any of the street's lesbian former residents: artist Gluck (Hannah Gluckstein) had a studio at number 48 in the 1920s; Romaine Brookes, who painted Una Troubridge's portrait, lived at number 50, an imposing double-

fronted building with a 'deliveries downstairs' sign that looks all too contemporary; author Radclyffe Hall, Troubridge's lover, spent two years at number 56. (This is a good point to head off towards the Chelsea Physic Garden, see page 7.6, if you want to combine the two.)

A few minutes from Sloane Square, at the corner of Peter Jones department store, is Cadogan Gardens. Stride past the couples unloading forests of Harrods bags from their 4x4s and you'll come to number 97, home of Natalie Barney, hostess of a literary salon graced by Gertrude Stein, Edith Sitwell and Rainer Maria Rilke.

If you're still feeling energetic you could also seek out number 35/6 Sloane Street (the other end from Sloane Square) where Bryher (Winifred Ellerman) lived with the poet HD. If you're not, you might want to collapse in a coffee bar and ponder the shift from Chelsea to Hackney and the significance of the proposed new Underground line that will link the two.

UNDERGROUND Sloane Square

CARLYLE SQUARE
GARDEN LIMITED
RESIDENTS ONLY
NO DESTRUCTIVE BALL GAMES
NO LITTER PLEASE · NO DOGS

pink plaques

Hall Carpenter Archive

It's not always easy to find documentation of lesbian lives, so the Hall Carpenter Archive – a resource for information on all aspects of lesbian and gay existence, named after Radclyffe Hall (see page 3.8) and Edward Carpenter (see page 7.18) – is invaluable. The collection is divided into two: the print collection housed at the London School of Economics library comprises magazines, leaflets and other ephemera mainly relating to the period from the mid-1970s to the early 1990s; and the National Sound Archive at the British Library, which holds taped interviews with lesbians and gay men of all backgrounds and ages. Some of these were used in *Inventing Ourselves*, the Hall Carpenter lesbian oral-history book (there's also a gay men's equivalent). Since the British Library is not a public library you have to demonstrate a need for the 'unique resources of a national research collection'. Call them for advice. To access the LSE collection, call and make an appointment – but it's a good idea to allow twice as much time as you think you'll need.

ADDRESS literature at Archive, London School of Economics, Portugal Street, London WC2 (020 7405 7686); sound at National Sound Archive, British Library, 96 Euston Road, London NW1 (020 7412 7440)
OPEN LSE: Monday to Thursday, 10.00–19.30, Friday, 10.00–17.00; National Sound Archive: Monday, Wednesday, Thursday, Friday, 9.30–18.00; Tuesday, 9.30–20.00; Saturday, 9.30–17.00
ACCESS LSE: open access; NSA: access to British Library readers
UNDERGROUND Holborn/Euston

Highgate Cemetery

The cemetery opened in 1839 – when visiting the dead was considered to be a morally uplifting pastime – and was constructed to provide the extra burial space for a population swollen by the influx into London during the industrial revolution. In 1975 the Friends of Highgate Cemetery was founded to bring the overgrown and dilapidated site back into use as a 'social history museum in a nature reserve'. Its 37 acres are divided by Swain's Lane into two parts: Highgate West and Highgate East. There are more than 167,000 people buried here in more than 52,000 graves in both consecrated and unconsecrated ground – but you can still buy a burial plot for £3000.

The most famous occupant of the eastern side of the cemetery – where you can wander unguided – is Karl Marx, who boasts an appropriately imposing grave close to, and probably as the founding member of, the cemetery's 'activists' corner'.

On the western side access is restricted to group tours, and the Friends stress that this is an active burial ground and Grade II-listed park, not a tourist attraction – though it's one of London's finest. The guides each have their own interests so the tour is always different, and seasonal changes have a big impact too (spring, for snowdrops and bluebells, and autumn, for mists and shadows, are the best times to visit).

It is here that Radclyffe Hall – known as John to her friends – whose classic lesbian novel *The Well of Loneliness* was banned under the Obscene Publications Act when it was published in 1928, is entombed, along with the remains of Una Troubridge and Mabel 'Ladye' Batten, two of her lovers – how's that for hanging on to your ex-girlfriends? Their vault, with pillars and room for four bodies, is the size of a small chapel, in a curved 'street' of catacombs. (Burial in vaults above ground had become fashionable because of the fear of being buried alive.) Mabel's

name is chiselled above the cast-iron gate, and there is a brass plaque with the inscription: 'Radclyffe Hall 1943, And if god choose I shall but love thee better after death, Una.' The reality of her resting place wrecked my image of John's grave being tended by many small sapphic hands amid cow parsley and nettles. Sandblasting her vault doesn't have the same appeal.

ADDRESS Swain's Lane, London N6 (0181–340 1834)
OPEN eastern cemetery: April to October 10.00–17.00 (weekends 11.0–17.00), November to April 10.00–16.00 (weekends 11.0–17.00); western cemetery, tours only: weekdays 12.00, 14.00, 16.00 (15.00 in winter), weekends on the hour from 11.00–16.00 (15.00 in winter); no weekday tours in December, January or February
ACCESS £1 eastern; £3 western
UNDERGROUND Archway

Soho Gay and Lesbian Walk

The walk begins on the steps of St Martins-in-the-Fields, a church at the forefront of the debate about gay clergy, and close to South Africa House, the embassy of the only country apart from Ecuador where lesbian and gay rights are enshrined in the constitution. It ends at Old Compton Street, which our guide claimed had been a 'nothing street' before the influx of gay businesses. This suggests a very short memory. Some pre-Queer Street concerns still persist: the street reflects the presence of the local Italian community and the sex industry, part of Soho since the 1950s which both had a strong pre-pink-pound existence and will doubtless last beyond the street's current pink incarnation.

Asked why Soho had become a gay mecca, our guide put forward a 'melting pot' theory: the area that welcomed Huguenot and Chinese immigrant populations was also hospitable to gays. Another less rose-tinted thesis is that Soho's history as a home for bohemians, sexual deviance and prostitution attracted gay people keen for the safety of anonymity.

We move on to Charing Cross, where in the seventeenth century 'mollies' (the preferred term of abuse after 'sodomite') were punished in the pillories if they escaped hanging. In front of the station is a nineteenth-century replica of the cross of Eleanor of Castille, mother of Edward II (1284–1327), the gay monarch about whom Derek Jarman made the film of the same name.

A wealth of information is divulged about the les/gay theatrical world: the Coliseum where Cole Porter's *Kiss Me Kate* debuted; the Duke of Yorks where Noël Coward first went on stage in *Peter Pan*, opposite the aptly-named Brief Encounter bar; the Dominion where Judy Garland charged £1 for her one-woman show so that her fans could afford the tickets; the As You Like It coffee bar in Monmouth Street, frequented by

3.14

Quentin Crisp and Lindsey Kemp; the Queens' Theatre on Shaftesbury Avenue where Marlene Dietrich twice did a show.

There's so much information – she lived here, a bookshop or a secret 1950s club there – it's almost a relief to head back to Old Compton Street and the offices of Kairos in Soho, organisers of the tour. A non-denominational spiritual group for gays and lesbians, Kairos (the time of fruition) was set up in 1996 by a Methodist minister as an alternative to the commercial scene. The organisation also runs workshops and meditation groups including a weekly Women's Voice group.

The walk passes sites of mainly gay, rather than lesbian, interest because, our guide said, the information comes from criminal records, and lesbianism was never criminalised in this country after Queen Victoria famously decreed it could not exist. This slant is a disappointment – and a cop-out – but the walk, of around $2^1/_2$ hours, is fascinating for anyone interested in London and gay history, and gives Londoners the unusual experience of being tourists in their own town. To cheer up the women in the group our guide told us about a passing woman, bigamously married eight times, who was the scourge of the countryside.

pink plaques

ADDRESS organised by Kairos, 56 Old Compton Street, WC1
(020 7437 6063)
OPEN weekly on Sundays, 15.00–17.30
MIX lesbian and gay
ACCESS £5 strongly suggested donation
UNDERGROUND Charing Cross

pink plaques

bars and cafés

Bar Fusion

When this bar opened in the summer of 1999 a large sigh of relief was heard: 'Phew, now we don't have to walk all the way to the Angel anymore', and, 'At last we've got an alternative to the Angel'. Very soon, no one did walk the extra way to the Angel and after more than 15 years as a mixed gay pub, it has become a straight pub. Nobody seemed overjoyed by Bar Fusion itself – inside it's narrow, not unfriendly but with a low lesbian quotient (far lower than the now-missed Angel, although there is Eruption, a lesbian 'disco' on the first Saturday of the month) and not comfortable. In an age of heavily designed bars, Fusion is minimal rather than minimalist.

There's the 'stick a rainbow flag on it and we'll drink anywhere' contingent, relieved by this option, now that Islington has become Consumerville, stuffed with largely forgettable bars-with-bouncers, and the dissenting, 'I'm not going in there, it looks like a pound shop' attitude. Bar Fusion is even more reviled than the Angel was – in fact you'd think Fusion was solely responsible for the latter's demise. Of course, if there were more than two mixed gay bars in Islington there wouldn't be this level of hostility. But we probably wouldn't want to go there anyway. Sigh.

A poodle clamped under an arm and a Go-Ped (poodles have very short legs) caused the most excitement on our visit. Poor Bar Fusion, it's just a bar, it's OK. Some people you just can't please.

ADDRESS 45 Essex Road, London N1 (020 7688 2882)
OPEN daily, 13.00–24.00
MIX gay and lesbian
ACCESS open
BUSES 19, 38, 73 UNDERGROUND Angel

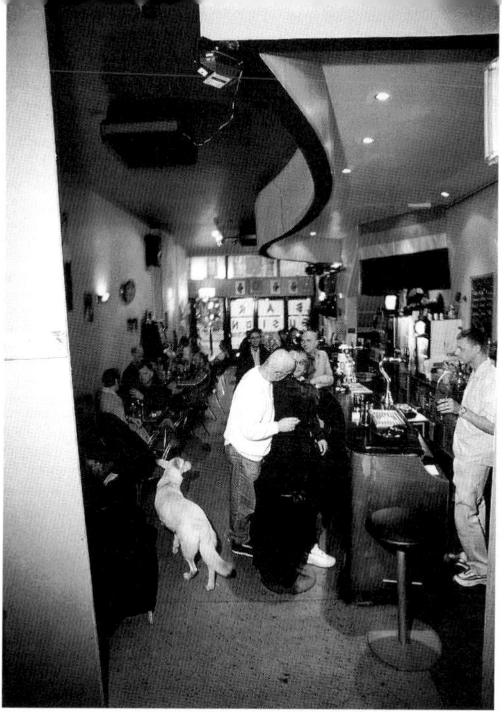

The Black Cap

A long-established drag pub, the Black Cap has always had a reputation for being totally unreconstructed, so it's a surprise to see how popular it is with lesbians. There's around 25 per cent women here, which is higher than you find in many a 'mixed' bar. As Jacky Clune might say, do they like rape jokes or something?

The staff are friendly, maybe to offset the shock of the queer tax being levied in Camden Town: drinks are not cheap. It's something of a relief from the trendiness of Soho, though, very casual with a few suits. Upstairs you have a sense of being in a pastiche theatre bar with gay-Paree-style theatrical prints. The music's loud, mostly gay-musak like Boney M and Abba. The performance space downstairs opens later in the evening.

This isn't somewhere I'd come on my own, and it's not a place to go if you're uncomfortable with men cruising, although there's none of the hostility dykes often report in other cruisey bars. The roof-garden terrace comes as a pleasant antidote to the fussy decor inside: it's a large space very simply put together with climbing plants hanging down, and it could be a good place to spend a summer evening.

ADDRESS 171 Camden High Street, London NW1 (020 7428 2721)
OPEN Monday to Thursday, 12.00–2.00; Friday and Saturday
12.00–3.00; Sunday 12.00–15.00, 19.00–23.30
MIX lesbian and gay, mainly men
UNDERGROUND Camden Town

Blush

By the time you read this Blush, which opened in April 2000, will probably be entrenched as a popular dyke venue in Stoke Newington. The owner, who used to run Due South down the road (see page 4.14), has a 20-year lease on the place, and, freed from the constraints of pleasing a brewery, is going for an over-25s crowd. She wants Blush to be a hear-yourself-talk place. Very novel.

When we visited in its very early days – in fact turning up very inconveniently just after opening time the night after a big party – we got a good welcome and there were plenty of people arriving for an early Sunday evening drink, with some walk-by trade. Maybe the Stoke Newington factor (see page 1.6) is going to spread to the north side of the high street.

Downstairs are sofas and a pool table; lesbo pulp fiction covers provide good reading matter on the inside of the toilet door. Home-cooked food of the organic persuasion is planned along with weekly jazz nights from the likes of Laka Daisical, events by the Emma Peel Fanclub, exhibitions on the walls, and occasional DJs playing ambient easy-listening sounds, presumably for those delicate over-25-year-old ears. Blush has all the signs of being in tune with the area.

ADDRESS 8 Cazenove Road, London N16 (020 7923 9202)
OPEN daily, 17.00–24.00
MIX mainly women
BUS 67, 73, 76, 106, 149, 243

The Box

The Box is reborn; still a box shape, still box-shaped menus and boxes on the wall, but you don't feel like you're actually in one anymore because a major redesign has really opened out the space. It's painted in a light taupe putty colour, which is very restful – a good thing considering the usual decibel level of chatter, and it goes very well with the black, white and grey clothes favoured by most of the customers.

Apart from its clientele and the usual gay-tax drinks prices, there's little to distinguish this from any other elbow-to-elbow coffee-and-food stop, though the menu is more interesting than average and changes seasonally. Pavement tables seem like a good idea until you register the volume of the traffic.

The photograph of a male torso clad in Calvin Klein underpants with, in case anyone missed the point, a strategically placed large frothy cappucino may give you a little hint about the clientele expected here. You wouldn't be entirely wrong, but don't be put off: firstly, plenty of dykes do come here; secondly, staff are unfailingly friendly and act like you should be here, menu designer aside.

ADDRESS Seven Dials, 32–34 Monmouth Street, London WC1
(020 7240 5828)
OPEN Monday to Saturday, 11.00–23.00; Sunday, 12.00–22.30
MIX lesbian and gay
UNDERGROUND Leicester Square, Covent Garden

Candy Bar

The Candy Bar was the cause of much excitement when it opened in 1997: finally a seven-nights-a-week bar for the girls in the heart of Boystown. Now established in its new venue – a corner plot with large windows on two sides and pavement tables on the Batement Street side – it's the level of visibility which is groundbreaking. The idea of loads of dykes queuing on Greek Street to get in at the weekend is very pleasing.

Plenty of seating both upstairs and down gives the Candy Bar a more relaxed vibe than its previous incarnation, but might also have the effect of making it less cruisey. All is not lost though as a visit to the toilet still necessitates running the gauntlet. The toilets actually lock too (for the moment) but gaps above the doors could also circumscribe impromptu encounters, which the bar is famous for.

Different dance nights run in the basement bar – karaoke on Wednesdays; Princess Julia DJs on Friday nights, Slamma on Saturdays, Kinky D on Sundays. These change as interests move on, so check if you want a night out for something in particular. The Candy Bar is never slow to take up a new trend: Loose, the strip night at the Sunset Strip, is another of its productions (see page 5.28). Expect Soho prices and, as a bottles-only bar, it's not the place to go if you're in the mood for sinking a few pints. Enthusiasm for the Candy Bar remains undimmed, and it's still the only one of its kind.

ADDRESS 22–24 Bateman Street, London W1 (020 7437 1977)
OPEN Monday to Thursday, 17.00–1.00; Friday 17.00–3.00, Saturday 16.00–3.00; Sunday, 18.00–23.00
MIX women, gay friends as special guests
UNDERGROUND Tottenham Court Road

Candy Bar

The Drill Hall Women's Bar

The women's bar at the Drill Hall is an institution, and the rules say no shows on Monday nights to keep it so. Bars close so often due to other pressures that it's quite a shock to find one that has lasted for more than 15 years with a core clientele of regulars. Don't be put off by the fact that it's a theatre bar. Even though most of the customers look like lesbians, this has more of a feel of a women's than a lesbian bar – probably because in the Drill Hall's lifetime 'lesbian bar' has come to mean something else. For some it's a convenient place to meet before going on somewhere else, others are there for the evening, getting stuck into bottles of wine.

It's open from 17.30, the tables are all full by 19.00 – there's a happy hour from 18.30 to 19.30 – and the level of conversation drowns out the music: Police and Frankie Goes to Hollywood, to give some idea of the vintage. The walls, often showing artworks, are lined with posters for the current show with Jackie Clune on the evening of our visit, and there are Lesbian Line recruitment leaflets on all the tables.

The Drill Hall's programme frequently includes les/gay productions: Split Britches and Bloolips often perform here and this is the home of the all-women pantomime, an annual, love-it-or-hate-it event usually reworking one of the festive 'classics' – in 1998 it was *The Adventures of Robyn Hood* – with endless opportunities for gender confusion, where feminism rules and a lesbian always gets her girl.

ADDRESS 16 Chenies Street, London WC1 (020 7631 1353)
OPEN weekly on Mondays, 17.30–23.00 (wheelchair access)
MIX women-only
UNDERGROUND Tottenham Court Road, Warren Street

Due South

As is right and proper in the heartland of lesbian Hackney, 'mixed' at Due South usually means 90 per cent women, except on Thursdays when it's women-only. Next door to the infamous Stoke Newington police station may not be a location to inspire confidence – and the staff are noticeably strict about late entry and drinking up – but this is an extremely popular local bar, mostly though not exclusively with twentysomething lesbians.

The haçienda theme of the exterior is continued inside in a raised seating area fitted out with sofas and low tables. With bare brick walls, original tiling half way down both sides of the room and part of a mosaic floor remaining, Due South is a little like an excavated ruin, if not one down Mexico way. Sadly, the body outlined in paint on the floor – a casualty of waiting for a drink, perhaps – has now disappeared, and actually service is fast and friendly. The pool table does a roaring trade and as it doesn't operate a winner-stays-on system posing opportunities are sadly limited. The beer garden can be a refuge from board games, quizzes, singles nights, gaming machines, a big-screen TV and a hot and smokey atmosphere, but all these can part of Due South's attraction. The long-planned restaurant is now open on Sundays and, with something of a captive audience, is predictably busy.

ADDRESS 35 Stoke Newington High Street, London N16
(020 7249 7543)
OPEN Monday to Friday, 17.00–24.00; Saturday, 12.00–24.00;
Sunday, 12.00–23.30
MIX lesbian and gay; women-only on Thursdays
BUS 67, 73, 76, 149, 243

Duke of Wellington

A stalwart of the Hackney bar scene, the Duke has been going for more than ten years. It has now surfaced from its much needed renovation – and, compared with years gone by, a higher lesbian quota – but that was always part of its charm and it's still useful for a quick local drink. From the outside with its newish music hall colours of mauve and orange (better than it sounds), Venetian blinds slightly open – the All-Bar-One vogue for transparency never took off here – so that you can see the little blue lamps whose glow matches the paintwork, the Duke looks different. At least you can tell it's open, and the blue glow looks quite welcoming.

When you get inside though, it's really only the light fittings which have changed – and terracotta walls do not a great difference make. If you hate blond wood and stark interiors, this could be just what you're looking for – it's so far at the other end of the scale it barely registers. It's very relaxed, with all the usual delights such as bingo, quiz night, Sunday lunches, and lots of dogs. 'Still here, still queer' read the signs on wall which has the effect of making me feel rather old and mauldin instead of elated as I assume it should, but maybe it's the Guinness (which has always been good here).

ADDRESS 119 Balls Pond Road, London N1 (020 7254 4338)
OPEN Monday, 16.00–23.00; Tuesday to Saturday, 12.00–23.00;
Sunday, 12.00–22.30
MIX lesbian and gay
BUS 30, 38, 56, 277

First Out

First Out will go down in history as a pioneering example of the les/gay café – in its time a strong competitor for the longest wait for a cappuccino. It's no longer unusual – though regular refurbishment helps to retain its freshness – but it's still very popular.

The two-storey space is loosely divided into a ground-floor café and a basement bar, though you can drink alcohol upstairs or take your food downstairs – or the very amenable staff will deliver it to you, dicing with death on the perilously steep staircase – but smoking is restricted to the basement. The food is a mixture of standard sandwiches and cakes, and better-than-average meals. It can get cramped, but you can stay for hours. The unusually large space for printed matter means it's a useful stop for picking up gay press and flyers; the noticeboard covers the usual categories; and the walls are hung with exhibitions by gay and lesbian artists.

Friday night in the basement is the busy pre-club bar Girl Friday – brash, energetic and clubby. Youthful babes in short t-shirts – visible belly buttons a must – are much in evidence, though it's perfectly safe for those not possessed of flat stomachs. It's actually mixed, but the ceiling is so low it's best avoided by those over 5 foot 8. Plenty of women come on their own and plenty of them are not shy: looking, smiling, staring. If Friday night sees you ready to go rather than ready to collapse, Girl Friday might be a good place to start.

ADDRESS 52 St Giles High Street, London WC2 (020 7240 8042)
OPEN café: Monday to Saturday, 10.00–23.00; Sunday, 11.00–22.30; Girl Friday: weekly on Friday, 20.00–23.00
MIX café: lesbian and gay; Girl Friday: women, gay friends as special guests
UNDERGROUND Tottenham Court Road

Fridge Bar

Handily placed for the Ritzy cinema and Substation South (for Dirty Dishes or Queer Nation, the mixed gay club nights) this bar is the 1990s offspring of the Fridge next door, which runs various gay and mixed nights. It's an attractive venue, popular with a mixed gay/straight crowd of cool Brixtonites, with a licence until 2.30 and reasonably priced drinks. It makes good use of an awkwardly narrow space but leaves little room for chairs inside, so be prepared to stand, though there are chairs and tables on the pavement if you want to sit by the main road.

In the main bar upstairs the music – soul classics, Sly and the Family Stone, Curtis Mayfield – is loud so it's not the place for a cosy chat. The basement dive bar opens at 22.00 and the djs play louder and heavier sounds until 4.00: like wkd in Camden and the Candy Bar (see page 4.10) it straddles the divide between bar and club.

ADDRESS 22 Town Hall Parade, Brixton Hill, London SW2
(020 7326 5100)
OPEN Monday to Wednesday, 10.00–23.00; Thursday, 10.00–2.00;
Friday and Saturday, 10.00–4.00
MIX gay and straight
UNDERGROUND Brixton

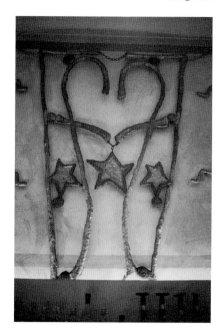

The Glass Bar

The Glass Bar occupies one of the listed gatehouses at Euston station, built in 1870. When the bar opened people described it as far bigger than it looks from the outside, and I imagined Dr Who's Tardis. It is more spacious than you would expect, but not up to intergalactic standards. You have to knock to gain entry, but once the door is opened you're immediately propelled into the action. You can tell newcomers by the look of surprise on their faces, their requests for pints in a bottles-only bar and by their reaction to the redoubtable Elaine, who gives great, not to say flirtatious, welcome, and seems to know everyone.

More than 6000 women have become members of this comfortable and friendly space since the doors opened in 1996. The Glass Bar stands as a popular stalwart of the bar scene, close to public transport in an area of more than 500 CCTV cameras – transport and safety were Elaine's priorities in her search for premises. Sofas and armchairs, always full, set the tone: this is a bar for sitting and chatting, not for prowling. Unfortunately the building's listed status means there's no possibility for extending the rather limited toilet facilities upstairs. Special nights – including Wednesday Child indie night, Singles Mingle on Thursday, Friday jazz nights with live performances, a pre-club night on Saturdays, and Mellow Jam on Sundays – and parties at significant points in the year attract a mixed, women-only crowd.

ADDRESS West Lodge, Euston Square Gardens, 190 Euston Road, London NW1 (020 7387 6184)
OPEN Tuesday to Friday, 17.00–late; Saturday, 19.00–late; Sunday, 14.00–19.00; no entry after 23.00
MIX women-only ACCESS £1
UNDERGROUND Euston

Liquid Lounge

Commonly known as the Popstarz bar, or by older patrons as the 'place that used to be the Bell', the Liquid Lounge is only a block away from Popstarz (see page 5.32), hence its Friday night 'Official Pre-Popstarz Piss-up' slogan. The Liquid Lounge, not to be confused with the more upmarket, designery bar of the same name in Westbourne Grove, is really a downscaled version of the club. Friday night sees an easy-indie playlist in the back bar – with sofas and a few tables, and a bigger dancefloor than many places that are officially clubs – to get you in the mood, though it can be a good night out in itself. The long-running Mis-Shapes on Saturday nights is really more of the same: a mixed bar/club playing indie, alternative pop and funk.

Club Deb – named after Debbie Smith, she of Elastica, Sports Bra and Curve fame, one of the DJs – is the Thursday-night fixture, a dance-music-free zone, but with plenty of music to dance to. With cheap drinks promotions, indie, funk, retro, rap, reggae, Club Deb is mixed but much frequented by girlz who like Popstarz.

ADDRESS 275 Pentonville Road, London N1 (020 7837 3218)
OPEN Thursday, 17.30–2.00; Friday, 17.30–1.00; Saturday, 17.30–3.00.
ACCESS Thusday £2 after 22.00; Friday free before 20.00, £3 before 22.00, then £5/£4 with flyer
MIX gay and lesbian
UNDERGROUND King's Cross

Oak Bar

The Oak Bar went through a long process of refurbishment, which may have been one reason why attendance fluctuated along with the general vibe, which could shift from friendly, low-key, local to miserable last-chance saloon. All that now seems to be past. With its bistro-ish decor, purple and red lamps, and, of course, sofas, the Oak seems more comfortable with itself, with a couple of well-established club nights, Viv's Quiz Night (an institution in itself), and new ideas regularly being tried out.

Girlfriend is a women-only night with commercial dance and garage, and commercial dancers too. The night we visited it was busy enough but didn't really make the shift from bar to club. Given that, the go-go dancers seemed a little marooned; one in fluorescent white underwear and a stetson later became the Tequila Slammer girl, and one of the Loose dancers (see page 5.28), at the other sartorial extreme, remained swathed in veils.

liberté, now at the Oak after venues in Stoke Newington and Finsbury Park, has long had a devoted following. It continues to live up to its quickly won reputation as a relaxed and cruisey night, serving up easy-groove soul and swing, club classics and some heavier garage and reggae sounds to a friendly dancefloor, and attracting an unusually good mix of black and white dykes. liberté hits the right note for a lot of women: it has hung on to its local feel, and plenty of people travel across town for it.

ADDRESS 79 Green Lanes, London N16 (020 7354 2791)
OPEN Monday to Thursday 17.00–24.00; Friday 17.00–2.00; Saturday 13.00–2.00; Sunday 13.00–12.00
ACCESS liberté 21.00–2.00 last Saturday in month, £3 before 22.30, then £4; Girlfriend 21.00–2.00, weekly on Friday, free before 22.30, then £3
MIX lesbian and gay; Girlfriend and liberté women-only
BUSES 73, 141, 171, 236,

The Oval Theatre Café Bar

The Oval Theatre, beside the cricket ground, has a long record of producing lesbian and gay theatre, particularly new work, but it's always had a fairly low profile. The Oval also shows work by lesbian photographers from time to time, so it's worth looking out for publicity to see what they're up to. In autumn 2000 the Oval premiered Stephen Luckie's new play *Junior's Story*, sequel to the successful *Talking*. At the time of writing the rest of the programme was unconfirmed but its commitment to lesbian and gay work makes it worth checking out the listings.

With two theatre spaces and dance studios with sprung floors and glass ceilings, there's a lot going on here; the theatre is hoping to get Lottery funding to upgrade the premises – if it's successful Greae will become the resident theatre company and the whole place will be made accessible to performers (and spectators) with disabilities.

It's a touching reminder of days gone by that you can still reserve seats here without prior payment – The Oval has that kind of feel about it and it's not unpleasant. The bar/café area, where you can order food as well as drinks, both at cheap prices, is bright and friendly, and lo-fi to the extent of the music box perched on a stool in a corner.

ADDRESS 52–54 Kennington Oval, London SE11 (020 7582 0080)
OPEN Monday and Tuesday, 18.00–20.00; Thursday to Sunday, 18.00–23.00
MIX gay and straight
ACCESS depends on performance
UNDERGROUND Oval

Vespa Lounge

The Vespa Lounge has succeeded in creating something almost unheard of in lesbian history: a reasonably stylish, relaxed bar in an interesting space, despite being given only a month and a tight budget by the brewery Allied Domecq to redesign and redecorate. Two years on, Vespa is well established and busy with a programme of special nights including the comedy night, Laughing Cow/Hersterics (see page 5.26).

Underneath the infamous Centrepoint building at Tottenham Court Road, opposite First Out (see page 4.18) and St Giles' Church, inevitably a certain competition has grown up with the Candy Bar (see page 4.10) and despite losing on floorspace and opening hours (soon to be extended), Vespa wins on attitude, or lack of it. A recruitment policy that put friendliness as an essential rather than an optional quality shows as staff keep their cool and stay on-message behind a bar that can only be described as compact.

Tables cover a third of the space, while the inevitable (and busy) pool table at the opposite end takes care of the dyke-herstory angle. Outsize silver pouffes are shared by a mix of women in Prada and Umbro, either out for the evening or for a pre-club drink.

ADDRESS upstairs at The Conservatory, under Centrepoint, St Giles' High Street, London WC2 (020 7836 8956)
OPEN Wednesday to Sunday, 18.00–23.00
MIX men as guests
UNDERGROUND Tottenham Court Road

clubs

Club K

Kenric, the lesbian social group that runs Club K, has always suffered from its image as a club for closeted, upper-class women of advancing years, a little like the lesbian chapter of the Women's Institute (what's wrong with a nice pot of jam anyway?). This may once have had the ring of truth about it – Kenric was set up in the 1960s – but now the organisation is being dragged into the twenty-first century, and Club K is evidence of that.

'Not tea and scones, not twinset and pearls,' it's three floors of entertainment – more a social night than a club – in a pub close to Fleet Street. The basement disco plays a mix of retro and new music (by DJs CJD Mad Cows); upstairs is pub space for sitting and chatting and drinking and where newcomers are welcomed, though most come with friends and/or girlfriends; on the first floor there's a pool table. If this is your scene, what more could you want?

Well, for a start some members have complained that they want a hard floor not carpet to dance on, a small request with big implications, necessitating a move to a club space and all that entails. Obviously the new publicity is working – plenty of women here would have looked equally at home in any of the more sceney venues around. The usual smattering of tattoos and piercings is coupled with big hair: it's a very mixed bag.

Kenric's strengths are its nationwide presence and its motto, which promises that it is 'for all women', well, all lesbians. It aims to offer – don't they all? – an alternative to the scene, in this case one that isn't 'cruisey and hard'. Plenty of dykes, even in London, want what Club K provides, carpet or not: Kenric's national membership is more than 2000, with an average age of 35 – not 70 as its publicity officer was keen to point out.

Club K

Aside from the monthly Club K, Kenric organises four major events in London each year including Christmas and Valentine's Day celebrations and a boat trip on the Thames, as well as local sports activities, wine tasting, concerts, discussion groups and gardening clubs. Confidentiality is still a watchword, and the assurance that all Kenric correspondence is sent under plain cover is a stark reminder that times are not as enlightened as we might assume.

ADDRESS The Cheshire Cheese, Little Essex Street, London WC2
OPEN monthly on last Saturday, 19.30–23.00
MIX women-only
ACCESS £4/£2 concessions
UNDERGROUND Temple

Club V

Originally called Vaseline until legal action was threatened, Club V is home to an alternative gay and indie scene. Self-styled 'queerest of the queer', determinedly marginal and with a devoted following, it's best described as a left-field Popstarz (see page xx) with a more inspired play-list and live music. It's really more of a gig than a club, on the wrong side of Islington and suitably scuzzy for the home of queercore (hardcore meets queer).

Although it's been going slightly longer than Popstarz it's taken a very different route: widespread popularity would not constitute progress for Club V, involving as it would appropriation by the scene which its repu-tation is built on critiquing/despising. The organisers use the door money (bar receipts go to the Mean Fiddler which owns the space) to pay for bands, records and expenses; there's no gay profiteering here.

Research assistant of the evening said that everyone looked geeky, which may be a little harsh, but it's definitely a relief from the relentlessly designer-led scene. There's no style fascism here; it's more of a DIY ethic. Be prepared for wild dancing and even a spot of pogoing. And horizon-broadening sounds: Club V puts the indie back into indie so much so that entrenched musos that we are, or were, we could recognise only one Jesus and Mary Chain song all night.

ADDRESS upstairs at The Garage, 20–22 Highbury Corner, London N5 (020 7607 1818)
OPEN fortnightly on second and fourth Saturday, 21.00–3.00
MIX lesbian and gay
ACCESS £3.50/2.50 with flyer/£2 concessions
UNDERGROUND Highbury & Islington

Duckie

For most of the evening Duckie operates as a trash club specialising in 1970s and 1980s music. And don't we all love dancing to Gordon Giltrap and Elkie Brooks, and indeed to most of the discs that the expressionless, fright-wigged Readers Wifes [sic] care to spin – there's plenty of indie and soul thrown in with the trash. This happy state of affairs (not for everybody, though – some newcomers look mystified when they walk through the door, often to be greeted by cadaverous comedian the Divine David) is then interrupted, but not too often, by performances.

Chloe Poems is a favourite, as is Jackie Clune, the chick with flicks and a good line in Karen Carpenter singalongs, while Amy Lamé presides regally over it all. Chloe Poems, clad in his trademark gingham dress, delivers 'The Queen Is Satan's Boyfriend', one of his appealingly-titled frenzied recitations.

The Vauxhall Tavern became a gay pub after the Second World War but dates from 1863, built on the site of the Vauxhall Pleasure Gardens, a performance venue for orchestras, firework displays, acrobatics and, apparently, the original bearded lady. In 1998, in response to a leisure- and shopping-centre proposal that would involve demolishing the Vauxhall Tavern, Amy Lamé organised a campaign – remember gay politics? – to get the building listed. Given the popularity of facial hair as a lesbian conversation topic, the pub must be saved.

Duckie is definitely big fun, though the Vauxhall Tavern, listable or not, is not. Lesbians are a little thin on the ground. A Friday-night Duckie and Artskool, another Duckie production, at the Connaught Rooms which attracted a lot more women disinclined to brave Vauxhall on a Saturday night are unfortunately no more, but Duckie is a movable feast – to any licensed premises, alcohol (in copious quantities) being the stimulant of choice here – and given to new incarnations and

Duckie

seasonal specialities (see Post-pride, page 2.12).

Like Popstarz (see page 5.32), Duckie has become very much part of the scene – despite starting from the position of adopting a critical attitude towards it and setting out to offer something quite different. It's called co-option, kids.

ADDRESS Vauxhall Tavern, 373 Kennington Lane, London SE11 (020 7582 0833)
OPEN weekly on Saturday, 21.00–2.00
MIX lesbian and gay
ACCESS £4
UNDERGROUND Vauxhall

Exilio

Ritualised sex on the dancefloor, Latin music and a cheap bar are Exilio's defining features. Other than that, it's really up to you and the DJ. The music is mainly salsa and merengue; there are a lot of hoofers who know the steps and many who've clearly been religious about going to classes, but it doesn't matter if you haven't. Exilio is a club for enjoying fancy footwork, your own and other people's: you could experience it all as performance if you don't want to take part yourself. It's not relentlessly goodtime music – some Lat/Am power pop is in there too – but it's all sound dancing material, enough to lift the most benighted soul.

Exilio is mixed on every axis: flexisexual, English- and Spanish-speaking (all signs and announcements are bilingual), widely varying ages, trannies and leathermen, macho women and queeny boys. Advertised as 'a temple of Latin music', it's in a hotel basement – but it's not the surroundings that count, it's the worship. Take your partners.

ADDRESS 229 Great Portland Street, London W1 (0956 983230)
OPEN fortnightly on Saturday, 21.00–3.00
MIX lesbian and gay
ACCESS £6
UNDERGROUND Great Portland Street

FIST

'You're a virgin, aren't you?' dynamic mistress of ceremonies Suzie Krueger kept asking people coming into the club, often the ones in jeans looking tentative. It could have been me, a first-timer on several counts: FIST, rubber dress, fetish club. Quite a Saturday night then. But as is often the case on such occasions, the anticipation outweighed the event.

Inside, the lighting is dark rather than low, and the whole place is swathed in camouflage netting. There's hard music, there are wall-to-wall bare arses and shaved heads, there's an upstairs backroom and there are sex films. While I'm watching one there's a conversation behind me about conveyancing that could have graced any dinner party, any night, and this was said to be a wild night. What happened to the bacchanalian orgy we feared and hoped for?

Although the dress code is said to be, um, strict, a fair number seemed to have gained entry wearing t-shirts and spiked leather collars – it's like part-time punks all over again. In the sea of harnesses, head restraints, leads, collars and handcuffs few outfits stood out except a matching chainmail vest and executioner-style mask that could have held its own on any couture catwalk. For aficionados SM may be about testing physical and emotional limits and acting out profound anxieties about the body and psyche; for the voyeuristic visitor it looks like a dull club whose once shocking uniforms have become commonplace.

No chance of being shocked and appalled, then. Only the doorman in full army fatigues cradling a gun managed a severe challenge to liberal/aesthetic sensibilities. More interesting was the range of bodyshapes and ages: here is a place where men, at least, can be out and old and fat.

Suzie Krueger – who orchestrates the whole shebang from the front box – was also responsible for the women-only Clit Club, but got bored with doing a single-sex night so set up FIST five years ago, in theory, at

least, a ground-breaking 'sleaze pit for dicks and clits'. She seeks out sleazy venues for her clubs, and this alley off a backstreet in Camberwell is just right.

The most exciting thing that happened all night (apart from the girly business of dressing up) was the huge fuss caused by a man who was accidentally photographed as we were capturing our outfits for posterity – definitely not for publication. In a month that had seen three cabinet ministers outed we were hoping for an MP at least, or a senior civil servant perhaps. We should have rushed to a 24-hour film-processing lab – but it was late so we got into the car feeling disappointed and jaded and went home.

ADDRESS Imperial Gardens, 299 Camberwell New Road, London SE5 (entrance on Medlar Street); EMAIL suzie@panther.netmania
OPEN monthly, check press for day, 22.30–6.00
MIX lesbian and gay
ACCESS £10, dress code strictly leather/rubber/uniform/PVC
UNDERGROUND Oval
CAB gay cab firm available throughout the night

Galore!

Galore!, not content with pioneering a big monthly event well outside central London, is trying to free lesbians from the tyranny of combat trousers and vests, and create a space where dykes feel free to speak out against housemusicism. Such are the promises of the Galore! for Mayor manifesto, and in the month before the London mayoral election Galore!'s candidacy seemed less laughable than most.

A leading light in the campaign for queer 'trashy splendour and disco naughtiness', for which there seems to be an insatiable appetite, Galore!, going for the goodtime rather than the trendy, has become something of a beacon in south-west London in the last couple of years. Punters so keen they're dancing before midnight shock! Dykes actually asking to be photographed for this book bombshell! Popular club in zone 3 outrage! North Londonists may find this all too much to cope with. Someone will probably set up a helpline.

Theatre bars may not be the most prepossessing spaces but as they go Waterman's lends itself well to a club. Charlotte Harris, one of the organisers, says people don't come to Galore! to pull, they come to meet their friends. But with everyone given a numbered sticker to wear and a messages board where you can flirt with the number of your choice without having to do it face to face, this seems unlikely. It's got to be a better bet than internet dating.

ADDRESS Waterman's Arts Centre, High Street, Brentford, Middlesex (020 8568 1176)
OPEN third Saturday of the month, 21.00 until late
MIX gay and lesbian
ACCESS £6/4 concessions
UNDERGROUND train to Gunnersbury, then bus to Brentford High Street

Gia

'As good as it gets' says the flyer for Gia women's nightclub in Islington, which sounds strangely mullish publicity for a club greeted with sighs of relief from punters not overburdened with choice in the area when it opened, early in 2000. You find Gia in a warehouse building behind the Caledonian Road with windows stretching its full length, a lovely wooden horseshoe-shaped bar in a room that's all dancefloor and several different levels – housing DJ, seating, waitress-service cocktail bar and restaurant area serving inexpensive gastro-pub food – overlooking it. Good it is.

The music is mainly off-the-shelf house and disco classics which will probably not thrill anybody but will keep everyone happy enough – and this is the team who once ran the popular Ginger's and Spats clubs so they know all about it. Gia attracts an easy-going, youngish crowd, obviously pleased with what they've got and happy to dance and hang out here. Each month Gia features a live act: Belinda Carlisle, Tanita Tikaram and Hazel Dean, all of whom will probably go down well here, are promised, as well as talent spots and celebrity book-signings.

Plans are afoot for a Friday night Bar Gia in the bar next door. During the summer outside tables – for once, in London, not ruined by traffic fumes – will make this an even more attractive proposition.

ADDRESS Shillibeers, Carpenters Mews, North Road, London N7 (020 7607 0519)
OPEN usually first Saturday in the month (phone to check), 20.00–3.00
MIX women only
ACCESS £5/4 concessions
UNDERGROUND Caledonian Road

Kali

Kali is a multi-racial, multi-sexual club playing Quwali, Bhangra, Hindi and Bollywood music – a mix that foxes those used to the repetitive rhythms of most gay-club turntables – with a sprinkling of club beats, courtesy of DJs Ritu and Rizwan. You walk in and walk straight on to the dancefloor after being welcomed with a handshake and a smile. Coaches bring the faithful from across Britain and people have even been known to come over on Eurostar, such are the delights to be had.

There's nothing special about the place itself (though it has a certain nostalgia value for those of us who used to come to gigs here). It's a barn-like room above a pub, with the usual nasty toilets, a few chairs and tables and a bar serving up rubbishy beer in plastic schooners.

A big video screen shows Bollywood dance routines then switches to Michael Jackson (or was it Janet?) – but this doesn't distract you for long from surveying the scene around you. There are people in drag, in combat trousers, in shalwar kameez; white-shirted medallion men dancing with others in embroidered saris; those who know what they're dancing to and those who just like it. People say sorry when they tread on you; unknown lesbians smile at you as a matter of course – and they're not necessarily on the pull and very probably not on E either. Bizarre. As clubs go this one seems fuelled by a natural high rather than pharmaceutical ones.

The Chutney Marys dance group – for whom no description could come close to adequate – brings a whole new meaning to men in dresses: drag queen goes to Bollywood. After their performance they move on to the dancefloor, giving a hard time to PVC-clad gay boys, who respond with a certain amount of audience participation.

Kali was set up in 1995, an offshoot of Shakti, which itself grew out of the social group of the same name for South Asian lesbians and gay

men and friends. Asia, the 1980s Islington club at Paradise (now The Complex) was a precursor of this.

The publicity says the club is for 'attitude-free connoisseurs' – which just about describes the punters. But luckily, just as I was imagining that I might be at one with all my sisters and brothers, all having a wonderful Friday night together, I met dyke-from-hell in the toilet, who either wanted my job or, as my research assistant of the evening thought, my phone number. So we left, exhausted and very sweaty, but with preconceptions intact. Phew.

ADDRESS The Dome, 1 Dartmouth Park Hill, London N19
OPEN first and third Friday, 22.00–3.00
MIX lesbian and gay
ACCESS £5/£3 before 23.00, £6/£4 after
UNDERGROUND Tufnell Park

Laughing Cows/Hersterics

As one of the comics said, 'shouldn't a lesbian comedy club be called "miserable cows"?', but Laughing Cow, launched early in 2000, was full of women intent on having a good time. So many, and such a good time in fact, that it seemed a shame that it's a Sunday night affair because early closing means the show finishes and it's all out, without an hour or so to capitalise on the atmosphere that develops during the evening.

Donna McPhail is MC and likely to be the best known on any night; though she only does short lead-ins it's worth going for her alone. Other names you might come across are Clare Summerskill, Shappi Khorsandi ('my father forced me into stand-up comedy') and Cathy P. It's a mixed night including male punters – though men seem to have had advance warning of the Femidom jokes and taken a raincheck – and straight comedians.

Lots of the comedy was heard-it-all-before stuff, standard subcultural, but no less funny for that. Long hair, lipstick, Spice Girls ('Posh Spice is so stupid she makes a footballer look clever'), serial heartbreak, short nails, ex-girlfriends, lesbian bed death ('you know it's come when you're doing tit-for-twatting'), getting older, best friend's girlfriend traumas – let nobody say that lesbians can't laugh at ourselves. Apart from slight disbelief at the contraception jokes the only sharp intake of breath I heard was during the one about Fred and Rose West: 'how long do you have to be with someone before you can tell them what you're really into?'

ADDRESS Vespa Lounge, under Centre Point House, St Giles Circus, London WC1
OPEN Sunday, 20.00–23.00
MIX mixed
ACCESS £6/5
UNDERGROUND Tottenham Court Road

Laughing Cows/Hersterics

Loose

'The more dollars you give her, the more clothes she takes off and she's got a sick mother,' says our emcee. 'Don't talk, don't touch, give it up for X, buy your dollars now, don't walk out in the middle of a routine if you're in the front row'. We do as we're told.

Take-up on the dollar-bill tips she sells starts slowly but gets quite fevered. Loose is a first for London, brought to you by the Candy Bar, who also intend to set up a website to expand the paltry selection of online lesbian sex sites. Even though it's become almost passé to find dancers in lesbian bars (see page 4.26), there is something significantly different about going to a real Soho strip joint. For a start, you know that's what happens here all day long, but you stop thinking about that quite quickly for obvious reasons. And you're not surprised to learn that the dancers prefer working the girly night even though the dollars might flow less freely because it's more of a laugh and there's no drooling, silent men to contend with.

There's no doubt it's fun and something of a turn-on, even if shaved cunts, sex-shop underwear, big girly hair and five-inch heels aren't your thing. I'll never underestimate the power of a nurse's uniform again. Most of the dancers wear a garter and/or a chain belt, making it easy to deposit your dollars without touching but pretty soon a trend starts for doing it mouth to mouth, and despite the 'no touching' rule, a lot of it does get by.

Once you've slaked your interest in the dancer dangling rhinestones from her labia (don't we all), laughed over the lezzy routine, been briefly astounded by the incredibly acrobatic possibilities involved in pole dancing and you're no longer shy about being so very very close to the stage, you might find your attention wandering. You could ponder the cost of such extensive hair removal and whether the

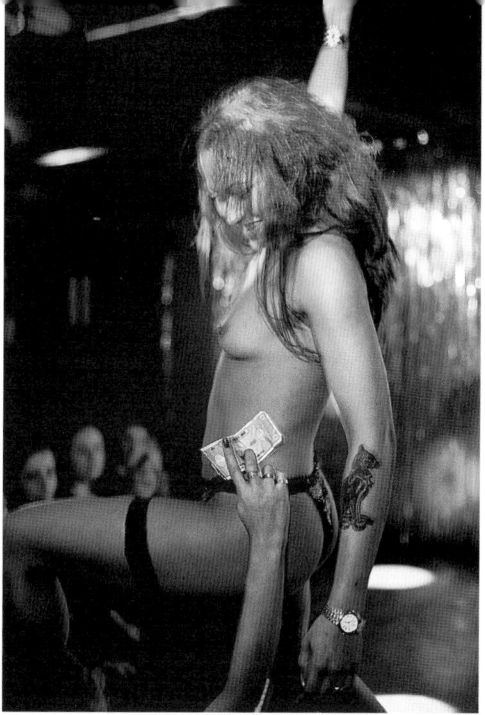

dancers' bras are fitted with some kind of easy-release catch cruelly kept secret from the general lesbian public. Now that really could be life-changing.

Some of the punters look like they've just come from a very straight office job and some are in dresses; two women probably in their 60s are enjoying themselves bigtime, and that's a sight not seen often enough on the scene.

ADDRESS Sunset Strip, 30 Dean Street, London W1 (020 7494 4041)
OPEN Tuesday, 20.00–1.00
MIX women-only
ACCESS members £6 before 22.00, then £8, £5 membership: ten visits equals one free entry, non-members £8 before 22.00, then £10
UNDERGROUND Tottenham Court Road

Popstarz

Popstarz has moved from alternative to mainstream as indie music became top of the Britpops. In its infancy, it was a delight for anyone underwhelmed by the pap served up as dance music in more commercial gay clubs. Now it's an institution but let's not get snotty about it – what's wrong with popular anyway? After six moves in its five years it's based now at the Scala, once an independent cinema – and host of one of the lesbian beauty contests in 2000 (see page 2.4) – which was finally forced into closure after an illegal screening of *A Clockwork Orange* (re-released after director Stanley Kubrick's death in 1999); only a block away from the Liquid Lounge, aka the Popstarz Bar (see page 4.24), should you wish for the total experience. It's largely a young, sweaty and trouble-free night where drinkers and E-heads co-exist happily. Popstarz, always a hard-drinking venue, now does it with a little style, courtesy of designers FAT, and it's hard to be nostalgic about sticky floors. Memorably 1980s austerity pop-r'n'b classic 'Nothing goin' on but the rent' seems so out of place in these surroundings it's the perfect track.

Despite its move up in the world, Popstarz has still got no side, it's very much itself and continues to attract a mixed crowd. In terms of age there's plenty of people who look like schoolfriends of Nathan from TV's *Queer as Folk*, and some who look like the programme's ageing scene queen Bernie. Too mixed for some: it's long been a scene cliché to object to the high proportion of (apparently) straight people, but there's little evidence of straight men hassling women, which was an occupational hazard at one time. Security staff are very hot on this and eject the guilty.

The upstairs bar looks out over The Common Room, the main indie dancefloor, and it's an experience not unlike watching planes taking off at an airport but maybe less anoraky (though geek chic is big at Popstarz).

Popstarz

clubs

Popstarz

From this vantage point, while you're sealed in listening to the trashy music (Abba, Weathergirls, Chic) from The Rubbish Room, the second dancefloor, everyone looks bizarrely unco-ordinated. Or maybe they just can't dance, or maybe you've had a bad pint.

The Common Room still has the Scala film screen in pride of place, sadly not showing the same calibre of film, and the camber of the cinema has been terraced with railings which makes for plenty of space to hang around. As clubs go this one has great sightlines, which is really what it's all about.

ADDRESS The Scala, 278 Pentonville Road, London N1 (020 7738 2336)
OPEN weekly on Friday, 22.00–5.00
MIX gay and straight
ACCESS concessions, £4 before 23.00, then £5; with flyer, £5 before 23.00, then £6; members, £5; the rest, £8
UNDERGROUND Kings Cross

Rumours

In those far-off days when wine bars and Covent Garden were fashionable places to be, Rumours might have seemed like a great name in a great place. But while it can't be said to stir up the same anticipation of a now sort of place these days, Rumours' publicity boast of 500 dykes was not far wrong. The Ace of Clubs, London's much-derided, much-frequented, longest-running lesbian club to date, late of Piccadilly, spawned this offspring in 1999, and it's doing very well.

You find the Minories Entertainment Exchange – a name revealing something of the joys to come – after a walk through a deserted City. You notice a small trickle of dykes going in the same direction and as you get close to Tower Hill, sure enough office-party music tells you you're in the right place. This is the kind of cavernous City pub which, left to itself, could be OK. It's in railway arches with vaulted ceilings but with bits of faux-gothic carving decorating the little booths where you sit, just in case you forgot you were in the heart of Heritage London. It's the kind of place that desperate office workers go to get insensible (surely there's a more welcoming park bench nearby?) and that sensible tourists would avoid like the plague experience which may well be round the corner. And, because it's a very important kind of place in the very important City, Rumours comes complete with lots of security people with ear pieces in case the President drops by.

Rumours has this to recommend it: it's very busy, it has a commendably broad age range and appeal with dykes in suits, dresses, smart casual, utility wear, leather-tan chic, chicks with real flicks. I think the drinks are quite cheap too – they need to be.

If the security people would allow you to stand looking over the heaving sunken dancefloor, you would probably get a sense of how the eternal fires of the underworld must look. It's not pretty. The music is

Rumours

what you might expect in a sit-com holiday disco: very crowd-pleasing, mainly singalongahouse, 'Living the Vida Loca' managing, by some satanic inversion of everthing that is true and right about the world, to become a high spot. Call me snobbish, call me self-hating, I can think of no fresher hell than this. No point in lowering standards, after all. It'll run and run.

ADDRESS 64–73 Minories, London EC3
OPEN 20.00–2.00, second and last Saturday of the month
MIX women only
ACCESS £5
UNDERGROUND Tower Hill/Aldgate

Teaze

A rainy night in Leytonstone isn't an auspicious start to checking out the Leytonstone scene. But when we got to Teaze, it didn't look like the balmiest evening would tempt anyone here on a weekly basis. It didn't help that the rain was such that you could get soaked walking from the car, but the half of The Britannia pub where Teaze is held isn't the most tempting prospect. A DJ was bravely pumping out the music to no one in particular and a go-go dancer still did her stuff and then tried to sell Tequila Slammers – one of the few occasions when it almost seemed like a good idea – and you could just about imagine that on a busy night this could be worth walking up the road for. Drawing a veil over the goddessy murals and faux-marble walls, the best thing is the pool table lit by ultra-violet light which makes all the balls look like they're made of soft rubber and in strange colours.

But it's not all bad. By the time the dry ice threatened to gas us with an overwhelming room-freshener smell, we'd discovered the much nicer bar. Local lesbians may not support Teaze, but they do support the pub, and you can see why. It's nothing wild but it's a pleasant-enough gay local with food and quizzes and Hybrid, an indie night, and evidently worth walking round the corner to, even in a downpour.

ADDRESS The Britannia pub, 493 Leytonstone High Road, London E11 (020 8539 0096)
OPEN first Friday of the month, 21.00–2.00
ACCESS £3
MIX women-only
UNDERGROUND Leytonstone

Vita's

Vita's – an easy, friendly night that began early in 1998 – specialises in interesting venues, and moved from the strange but attractive surroundings of the Central Club in Great Russell Street, to the London Lighthouse, the UK's first purpose-built Aids centre. It's independently run, not sponsored by brewery or membership, and money from the (very cheap) bar goes to Lighthouse.

Vita's fills the gap some over-35s complain about. If you find the scene too abrasive, too young, or too musically challenging, you might enjoy the niche Vita's occupies.

The move from central London may have had an impact on numbers, but Vita's is still very popular and the presence of regulars from across London and as far as Chesire, Cambridge and Brighton makes for a friendly evening. With the flavour of a houseparty or local disco, it's unthreatening and comfortable – which doesn't mean nobody gets off together. There's a general willingness to dance to anything, no fear of being uncool or looking daft – this is a place where people Do the Locomotion, Saturday Night Fever routines and dance to a remix of 'I Will Survive' among people who still like singing along to it. Britpop and dance music haven't happened as far as Vita's is concerned, and the punters love it. There's a huge mix of styles here and while it is mainly over-35s, this is no ghetto: there are younger and much older women too. Midnight closing may seem shockingly early but you can always go back into town.

The space, laid out with candle-lit tables bookable for birthdays and celebrations, would be recognisably a function room even if it weren't named the Ian McKellan Hall. One advantage of holding Vita's here is the Lighthouse's famous fragrant garden, to which you can gravitate during the summer. In winter you can still enjoy the conservatory space,

Vita's

excellent for peeking through palm fronds at an object of attention. Or failing that you can sit and chat and rest up from the rigours of the dance-floor. In a more club-type setting this would be known as the chill-out space. And Vita's may not be the most up-to-the-minute club London has to offer but it is a very relaxed space and a much-appreciated night.

ADDRESS 111–117 Lancaster Road, London W11 (07957 376270)
OPEN usually monthly, Saturday (call to check), 20.00–24.00
MIX women-only
ACCESS £6.50/£6.00 with flyer
UNDERGROUND Ladbroke Grove

tea dancing

Rivoli Ballroom

'Heaven, I'm in heaven
And my heart beats so that I can hardly speak
And I seem to find the happiness I seek
When we're out together dancing cheek to cheek.'

A spectacular 1940s frontage confronts you on the south-London high street. Inside, there's a wide stairway positively designed for making a grand entrance into the hangar-like space with mirrored struts on its domed ceiling. It's hung with an abundance of lighting – thankfully not all on at the same time – crystal chandeliers, mirror balls, giant red lanterns, something that looks like floodlights, and a string of red bulbs around the edge. Gas lighting survived here until the late 1980s.

The red-plush room was full of lesbians, gay men and children, in suits, ballgowns and leathers with a sprinkling of sequins and glitter and a few drag queens. On the dancefloor couples lived out their *Sound of Music* fantasies with a Viennese waltz. The music from the indefatigable Jacky's Juke Box, in front of the tinsel-hung stage, was hugely varied: Barry Manilow, the theme tune to *Upstairs Downstairs* and Junior Walker cropped up among the 1940s and 1950s classics. The dances are announced: 'This next one's a quickstep … actually it's more like a foxtrot.' Even line dancing looks impressive here with a ballroom full of queers.

It's all very decorous: people sit and fan themselves after a spin around the floor, there are no gaming machines, chewing gum is banned, and in the Ladies Boudoir, furnished with chairs on which to sit out unpartnered dances, women were changing into their dancing shoes. But not decorous enough for some apparently: the poppy-seller (it was Armistice Day the next day) confided that he liked to come dancing at the Rivoli himself, tea dancing

Rivoli Ballroom

but to 'something a little more formal'.

The Rivoli began as a music hall in 1850, became a cinema after the demise of vaudeville, and then in 1957 a ballroom, in its day hosting big-name bands and the likes of Acker Bilk, George Melly and Spike Milligan. Now the building is Grade-ii listed and a family business – beseiged with offers from developers and antiques dealers after the hardwood panelling, they're hoping for lottery funding to help with maintenance costs. The gay and lesbian tea dance is a monthly fixture in a full calendar, proof if any were needed that the Rivoli is 'not grab-a-granny, it's a living place'.

ADDRESS 350 Brockley Road, London SE4
(020 8692 5130)
OPEN monthly on first Saturday, 19.30–24.00
MIX lesbian and gay and local
ACCESS £3.50
BR Crofton Park

tea dancing

Waltzing with Hilda

The name tells you everything you need to know: Waltzing with Hilda is latin and ballroom-dancing fun. After a stint at the now-sold Central Hotel, Waltzing with Hilda is now upstairs at Jackson's Lane Community Centre in Highgate in a church hall where the DJ stands supreme beneath a huge stone arch, silhouetted against the back window. Other benefits of Jackson's Lane are that it's a 'more pro-dyke space and no one minds if you snog your girlfriend'; you can wolf down some food after taking part in one of the classes – beginners and improvers – early in the evening; and pub prices at the bar. Hilda's will hopefully be going weekly – monthly sessions aren't regular enough to remember any new steps.

If you get there early you can learn the steps, otherwise dance to your own on the sidelines, although you may feel you're not really entering into the spirit. Dance enthusiasts aside – and ballroom does seem to be a burgeoning scene-within-a-scene – Waltzing with Hilda is an easy place to go, especially for dykes put off by more mainstream clubs, whether because of attitude, dress, music or age. Plenty of women came and bumped into friends and others looked as if they had made some there. The diehard dancers have no problems with the incomprehensible – to the uninitiated – announcements from the DJ: 'This next one's a sway'; 'This one's a horseshoe.' Even, or perhaps especially, in a church building the restrained sensuality of formal dancing creates a charged atmosphere: 'my partner' takes on a whole new meaning. Is she is or is she ain't?

The classes are also a serious business: some people bring special dancing shoes (rubber soles to be avoided) and rosin their soles. The beginners' class was being initiated into the mysteries of the Argentinian tango. Although mastering it is said to be a lifetime's work, by the end of the session they are doing something more than vaguely reminiscent of the tango.

Waltzing with Hilda

After the classes are over, the lights are dimmed, and the space really comes into its own. Change partners and dance. And they do ask each other to dance, though some couples look as though they've spent a lifetime twirling each other in their arms, as rhumba follows quickstep follows waltz.

ADDRESS Jackson's Lane Community Centre, 269a Archway Road, London N6 (079 390 72958)
OPEN usually last Saturday of the month, 19.45–24.00; improvers' class 19.45; beginners' class 20.30; Café Vert, until 21.00
MIX women-only
ACCESS £6.50/£5.50
UNDERGROUND Highgate

cruising

British Library

Don't make the mistake of dismissing the library as a venue too serious and learned for anything as venal as sex. In the old library in the British Museum stories circulated about seductions over the Special Collections. They were probably untrue – certainly they always involved a friend's friend's ex-girlfriend – but tantalising all the same. Its reputation as a cruising ground can be put down to shared characteristics with more conventional spaces – low lighting and lack of opportunity to speak, in this case due to the silence rule rather than high decibel levels.

The story goes that it was the light in the reading room which made everyone look more than usually charming. In our (literary) dreams perhaps. The new library, with modern lighting designed to avoid shadows across monitors rather than plant alluring ones across faces – probably better for working, but less flattering to the skin – would benefit from a few myths attached.

In the absence of any encounters, you can busy yourself by exploring those parts of the much-maligned new building which are open to the public – café, restaurant, bookshop and exhibition space. The courtyard can be a useful central place to sit and relax, as long as there's not too much building work going on around it. If you have a library ticket you could even do some work, though for the first few visits it's hard not to be distracted by the building itself as you check out the spaces – I recommend Humanities 2, it's less frantic and a more manageable size.

The old library was delightful, unless you wanted to get a book in the near future. Now a notice on the desks reads: 'A sign on the desk will light up when your book is ready for collection.' Now that's what I call a system. It's not a bad place to work, but the layout of the desks, with rows back to back, makes it feel a little crowded and even more

difficult to concentrate in. The noise level seems higher than in the old place too, what with the clatter of laptop keys and the sound of tills opening (tills?). Still, it should help you to avoid snoring over your books and to stay alert in case of any offers of myth-making experiences behind the King's Library.

ADDRESS Euston Road, London NW1 (020 7412 7676)
OPEN Monday, Thursday, 9.30–18.00; Tuesday, Wednesday, 9.30–20.00; Friday, Saturday, 9.30–17.00
ACCESS public areas: exhbition space, bookshop, restaurant; ticket-holders: reading rooms
UNDERGROUND Euston, King's Cross

Chelsea Physic Garden

It doesn't seem such an outrageous expectation that this botanic garden in Chelsea should be the home ground of the appropriately tweedy or their modern-day equivalent, Goretexed gardening dykes, but they were away the day I visited, although our guide was definitely material for the category of 'women in sensible shoes'. Still, my gardens-specialist research assistant had seen Ellen De Generes holding court on the grass two weeks previously, which must count for something.

Lesbian visitors or not, this walled garden is one of London's lesser-known pleasures. It has a secret-garden feel to it. As you approach from the west along Royal Hospital Road you pass an unmarked door in the wall – guaranteed to make any lesbian of a certain age feel they're on familiar turf – through which you later exit. Turning the corner you find the small though signposted entrance in Swan Walk.

The garden was established by the Worshipful Society of Apothecaries in 1673 for the 'pursuit of horticultural excellence' to promote the study of botany for medical purposes. It is set on a 3.25-acre triangle, located close to the river at Chelsea Embankment to ease the importing of plants, and has a microclimate 4 degrees warmer than the rest of London. The garden collaborates with Glaxo Group Research in testing plant extracts; its leaflets estimate that 80 per cent of all drugs are derived from plant life.

Not surprising, then, that this is not a purely decorative garden of formal flower beds; in autumn it's all pleasantly overgrown as they wait to collect seeds. There are poisonous as well as curative plants, all well signposted. Among the most notable were squashes like beached landing craft, citrus trees, Ayurvedic plants for Indian medicine, a rock garden built on black volcanic rock, woad (which gives a blue dye as used by Boadicea to frighten off the invading hordes), and a gingko biloba, extracts of which feature on chemists' natural-remedy shelves. It's prob-

ably the oldest tree species in the world, remaining unevolved with the same leaves eaten by dinosaurs.

Much of this information comes from the helpful leaflet/plan provided, which highlights points of seasonal interest and includes gardening tips. It's also well worth joining one of the half-hour tours, which are both entertaining and educational. Our guide, firmly in the English-eccentric tradition, was a mine of bizarre anecdotes, including one about the plant that must have been used to make Jesus Christ's crown of thorns as it's the only thorn that bends.

Having taken a turn or two around the garden, perused the plant shop and exhibition and sat in the café, you pass through the small door and feel as if you've been expelled back into the real world.

ADDRESS 66 Royal Hospital Road, London SW3 (020 7352 5646)
OPEN April to October: Wednesday, 12.00–17.00; Sunday, 14.00–18.00
MIX mainly straight at present
ACCESS £3.50; students/unemployed/children £1.80
UNDERGROUND Sloane Square

Flirt

You might go to Flirt with fantasy fulfilment in mind: visions of lightly clad women offering chilled flutes of champagne, sexual favours and massage in a gleaming, tiled interior, or of erotic encounters with mysterious females unidentifiable through the thick steam. And though Flirt is advertised as a 'hot night full of surprises', you would probably be disappointed. So save the fantasies, go to Flirt and have a good time.

Stow your effects in one of the body-bag-like lockers, grab your two white towels and make your entrance. Your locker number doubles as your bar tab, so you don't need to carry anything around with you.

The main room is pleasant enough – warm orange walls, stone floors, arched brickwork, TVs, bank seating, big sofas – but then you're not here to inspect the furnishings. It is, of course, beautifully warm and there's a slight tang of chlorine from the jacuzzi. Aside from the huge 30-woman jacuzzi, there are two sauna cabins (room for 20), a steam room, piles of free papers and a massage room. Some women keep bikinis or shorts on and there's a bit of a 'whehey the girls' factor, rowdiness in the jacuzzi covering up embarrassment. The music is, surprisingly, quite soothing, mainly soul sounds. It's all scrupulously clean with the least scummy steam room I've ever seen.

It's all a bit loaded – the idea of a lesbian baths is, after all, pretty mind-blowing. So when someone said the steam room was 'quite an experience' I didn't realise she was talking about the temperature until I visited it – and, yes, it was very hot. Obviously how 'hot' Flirt is will depend on the lesbians there on the night; on this occasion most people seemed to have come with their girlfriends and the backroom, now discontinued, was used only by already established couples. The attraction of being naked and able to be sexual in a public place in ways most people take for granted is undeniable, but it's a shame more lesbians aren't interested in

exploring the possibilities of casual, anonymous sex, particularly considering the level of complaint about it.

The difference between this and a women-only sauna is that here you can be sure that the woman you're staring at is of the same persuasion as yourself. But if staring is as far as it goes, does it really matter? 'Girls who come together stick together,' Flirt's publicity once said, but we can cut the innuendo here. 'Hot chick seeking all-girl backroom action' is the theory – she may be out of luck. It's a very pleasant way to spend a Monday night and a good place to be sexy with your clothes off, but probably only with someone you're already being sexy with at home.

ADDRESS Covent Garden Health Spa, 29 Endell Street, London WC2 (020 7836 2236)
OPEN monthly on second Monday, 18.00–24.00
MIX women-only
ACCESS £10
UNDERGROUND Covent Garden

Highbury Fields Toilets

Research into women's use of public toilets by Women's Design Service in the 1980s revealed that this one on Highbury Fields used to be known as a cottage. Annoyingly, there was no detail about when or by whom, and while it was intriguing to discover that women do, after all, do That Kind Of Thing, there has been no subsequent confirmation of it. It may be a first, it may be apocryphal – but then a rumour may be all that's needed, and this is probably where you heard it first.

It's a small brick building with wooden porches set on the edge of Highbury Fields, between Barclays Bank and Highbury Pool, where you will without doubt swim with lots of lesbians. It opens only during the summer, the gates are locked 15 minutes before closing time, and, take note, there is a caretaker. So get down there, any day but Sunday – that really would be an outrage.

ADDRESS Highbury Crescent, London N5, just in front of swimming-pool entrance
OPEN April to October; Monday to Saturday, 9.30–18.30
MIX women-only
UNDERGROUND Highbury & Islington

ICA

The ICA (Institute of Contemporary Arts) is at the corner end of the Nash terrace on the Mall opposite St James's Park, and with its extensive programme of cinema, music, performance, club nights, exhibitions and talks there's often something worth catching here. Sexualities are definitely on the agenda: in the past the ICA has hosted Duckie club nights and an exhibition of the self-portrait work of Claude Cahun, a French photographer who, sporting a shaved head in the 1920s, prefigured a certain kind of contemporary lesbian identity about 50 years before the modern concept existed, and indeed before lesbians were called lesbians.

If there's nothing to see that takes your fancy, the bookshop and the bar (with a late licence and usually somewhere to sit) are worth checking out. Failing that, watch the procession of people, some of whom look as if they live here and a lot of others who look very busy doing something very important. It may be full of people fixated on black but it's generally an affable place rather than terminally cool.

ADDRESS The Mall, London SW1 (020 7930 3647)
OPEN bar: daily, 12.00–2.00; bookshop: daily, 12.00–20.00
UNDERGROUND Charing Cross

National Portrait Gallery

In a world light on dykons the National Portrait Gallery provides a reasonable headcount. The regular exhibitions are full of old favourites – personalities and portraits – and the special shows mean it's worth dropping in a few times a year. Every summer the npg hosts the bp Portrait Award, which often includes (commended) work by artist Sadie Lee, who sprang into the lesbian consciousness when she won the award with her butch-dyke Mona Lisa portrait.

The selections change, but in the twentieth-century gallery you might find portraits of Julie Burchill and Charlotte Raven; Dawn French and Jennifer Saunders; The Beverley Sisters; Annie Lennox; Emma Thompson; Tilda Swinton, star of *Orlando* and *Female Perversions* (highlight of the Lesbian and Gay Film Festival in 1997, see page 2.2); work by Maggi Hamblin including a self-portrait; and Germaine Greer by Paula Rego, a perfect pairing of artist and subject, with Ms Greer looking suitably witchy in bright red.

Upstairs are many portraits of and by the Bloomsbury group, whose famously incestuous pairings make contemporary lesbian relationship patterns look like models of restraint. These include Virginia Woolf by Vanessa Bell (her sister); Vanessa Bell by Duncan Grant (her husband) and his self-portrait; Lytton Strachey by Simon Bussey; Edward Carpenter, the libertarian socialist who shocked society by living with his working-class lover George Merrill, by Roger Fry; Ellen Terry, the greatest actress of her day and the mother of Edy Craig, lover of 'Christopher' St John who also had a brief and ill-starred fling with Vita Sackville-West (see page 12.12), by George Frederick Watts, her first husband and 30 years her senior.

Also here are Marie Stopes, pioneer of birth control; Amy Johnson, record-breaking aviator; Benjamin Britten and Peter Pears; Octavia Hill,

cruising

7.20

social reformer and repressed lesbian; and Emmeline Pankhurst, prominent suffragette and founder of the Women's Social and Political Union, which she allegedly set up in part to prise her lesbian daughter Christobel away from her lover, one Esther Roper.

ADDRESS St Martin's Place, London WC2 (020 7306 0055)
OPEN Monday to Saturday, 10.00–18.00; Sunday, 12.00–18.00
ACCESS permanent collection free; special exhibitions, price varies
UNDERGROUND Trafalgar Square

cruising

Photographers' Gallery

Photography aside, the Photographers' Gallery has other advantages as a central-London venue, namely a café at no. 8 and a bookshop at no. 5. If you're looking for a refuge from the relentless gayandlesbianness of Old Compton Street (see page 1.2), no. 8 could be ideal, which is not to say that the café is not frequented by an above average number of lesbians. What better place to hone your gaze to perfection? A stream of interesting-looking women of undisclosed sexuality pass through both doors, browse in the bookshop, buy postcards and eat very good sandwiches.

Large shared tables mean you won't be bored: you're never far away from someone else's conversation, a portfolio being examined, contact sheets being pored over. In slow moments you might try the exhibitions, highly variable but often worth a look.

Note to militant smokers: try the ICA instead (see page 7.16).

ADDRESS 5 and 8 Great Newport Street, London WC2 (020 7831 1772)
OPEN Tuesday to Sunday, 11.00–20.00
ACCESS free
UNDERGROUND Leicester Square

Women's Pond

The pond is a profusion of breasts, underwear and bits of swimsuits. Open-air swimming in murky but invigorating water on Hampstead Heath is appealing (only during heatwaves, except to the most hardy), but the main attractions are the opportunity for topless sunbathing and the other sunbathers. During hot spells at weekends and after work – last swim is at 19.45 – it's packed, but there's always room for one more body.

The rules ban alcohol, nudity, radios, pushchairs, prams, dogs and under-eights, and entry is restricted to competent swimmers. With one exception none of these is ever enforced – nobody actually checks you're carrying your 25-yards certificate or confiscates your tinnies. Periodically one of the women in red hats comes and remonstrates with knickerless sunbathers; the more hardline will occasionally complain about topless women sitting up – bare breasts being acceptable only in the prone position, apparently. Together with the hard toilet paper, this policing reminds you that this is a municipal space.

If your idea of refreshments extends beyond the ice-cream van at the top of the road, a short walk to the north across the heath brings you to the Palladian villa Kenwood House with a café (and Henry Moore sculptures) on the Hampstead Lane side. On summer evenings open-air easy-listening classical concerts (some with fireworks) are staged on the bandstand across the lake. You need a ticket to enable you and your extravagant picnic to join the epidemic of families in the enclosure – and with the new arrangements the music no longer wafts up the hill to the ticketless. To the south on the Gospel Oak side of Parliament Hill lies the Italian café, recommended for plates of pasta, coffee and cakes. The view across the city from the top of the hill is one of the best but watch out for low-flying kites. At the foot of the hill there's an open-air lido if you prefer chemical blue to pond water.

Women's Pond

While the pond is certainly cruisey and a great place to stare, nobody seems overly concerned about how they look. Hampstead matrons mix – well, share space with – diesels and everybody in-between. Taking off your clothes is always a great leveller but accents and shopping bags remain big giveaways. The rumours of poisonous pike are much exaggerated, but pike there are, probably lurking in the muddy edges where swimmers are not allowed to venture.

ADDRESS Ladies' Open Air Bathing Pond (off Millfield Lane), Hampstead Heath, London N6
OPEN daily; times change seasonally
MIX women-only
BR Gospel Oak

eating

Balans West

Earl's Court isn't what it used to be: although the Colherne, home of the clone, still looks slightly sinister from the street it is now frequented by lesbians, and Balans West, inviting from the outside, is positively welcoming. Urban gay ambience with a vengeance, then, and welcome enough after Ted's Place, a seedy-looking bar in West Kensington where we were met at the door by a man practically making the sign of the cross at the awful sight of two lesbians wanting to come in.

Balans West was much more of a mix than expected: people on dates, birthday parties, mixed couples, couples out with the parents, straight people, people reading in the corner. It's a warm-coloured, buzzy place, but not too noisy, the service swift and friendly, and it was very busy for a Monday night. The aluminium-frame conservatory at the back would be a good place to book for a big party. There's not much defensible space around the tables, though you could get quite intimate with the people beside you.

The menu covers many bases for all times of day and all levels of appetite from duck and ginger ravioli to full English breakfast. Note that smokers of herbal cigarettes are outlawed here, along with pipes and cigars (haven't they heard of cigar bars?). The manager couldn't or wouldn't tell me whether this was a coy reference to people smoking grass or whether the smell of Honeydews really did put people off their Bellinis.

ADDRESS 239 Old Brompton Road, London SW5 (020 7244 8838); also a branch in Old Compton Street
OPEN Monday to Thursday, Sunday, 8.00–1.00; Saturday, 8.00–2.00
MIX lesbian and gay
UNDERGROUND Earl's Court

Champagne Dining Club

The title of this book caused some consternation among the women at the Champagne Dining Club, who would probably be more at home in the 'gay lady' camp. Dykes, and especially butches, who would either be mobbed or ostracised, are what these upmarket singles come to club dinners – where they mingle and network at uptown restaurants – to avoid. Exclusivity, privacy and confidentiality are the keywords here; married women and women just coming out are among the membership, who work as barristers, lawyers, business owners, in corporate personnel, pr, or corporate marketing. If you travel from outside London the club can arrange suitable accommodation for you too.

Ingrid Walsh, the hostess, has been running monthly dinners for women looking for select dinner companions ('and maybe more') since early 1997, two years after setting up the same service for gay men. Now there's a choice of single-sex and mixed evenings, all attended by Ingrid. The torrent of wine keeps the conversation flowing – whether directed at flirting or networking.

You need to be more than solvent, as they say in the contact ads, to fund dinners like these a couple of times each month– at Le Gavroche, The Lanesborough, Vong's, for example – which come in at between £55 and £85 a head, in addition to the membership fee, but conspicuous consumption is what it's all about. You could see why members would prefer to meet outside the mainstream club and bar scene – a distinct lack of label compatibility. On the other hand, if you're in funds and bored with combat trousers, this could be your answer.

ADDRESS various restaurants (020 8696 0829)
OPEN two or three events per month
MIX women-only or lesbian and gay mixed events

eating

Fried Green Tomatoes

You won't get the Deep South food here you might expect from the name – in fact if you keep to the women's bar upstairs you'll only get a snack. Wise to the set-up at the Café Goya, where Fried Green Tomatoes is a fortnightly event, many women eat downstairs before making their way up to the women-only bar, which makes it a night-out place rather than somewhere you'd drop in for a swift drink. Straight couples come in and eat so you get to watch the realisation of who's at the next table, at all of the tables even, dawn across their faces. Food (mains £7–12) covers dinners – bangers and mash, pan-fried cod in chilli and lemon – and light meals, dips and salads, and the menu changes monthly.

This is a low-key, friendly bar with amiable staff, a welcome addition to an underwhelming south London scene. The conservatory tacked on the back of the bar was quickly occupied by a group settling in for the evening. Judging by the number of women who bumped into friends, and those who had already become regulars in the first few months of existence, Fried Green Tomatoes is a largely local affair. But don't be put off by that: it's relaxed and laidback, and although in the press they describe the place as attracting a 'mature' crowd, it's one which most unusually attracts all ages from 18–60 (one I chatted to and one I guessed).

ADDRESS Café Goya, 85 Acre Lane, London sw2 (020 7274 3500)
OPEN first and third Wednesday of the month, from 20.00
MIX women-only bar; straight/gay restaurant
ACCESS open
UNDERGROUND Brixton, then 10-minute walk

Live Bait

This isn't an ironic joke to do with lesbians being called fish, it's about food: good fish and seafood and happy memories of solicitous lesbian waitresses. Now there are men too, and I'd stake a sardine or two that many of them are gay. But who cares, anyway? The food's great.

The three interlocking rooms, one containing the bar and one comfortable booths, are tiled in gleaming black and white that manages not to be cold, though the hard surfaces mean it can get noisy, so go early evening or lunchtime. In the evening there's a choice between the pre-theatre menu and the main menu (mains from about £15, starters £6–8), which includes a full list of crustacea – cherrystone clams, cockles, winkles, crabs and lobsters – and daily specials.

The pre-theatre option gives you two courses for £15.50; I chose rock oysters followed by grey mullet with pak choi and nero (squid ink) mash. A bowl of prawns and choice of breads (slightly over-elaborate: carrot and spring onion; cinnamon, raisin and turmeric) appears to keep you amused while you decide what to order. The wine list is heavy on New-World offerings and a high proportion of it can be ordered by the glass. When the food arrives it's delicious – and it's on big glass plates, keeping up the fish-and-chip-shop idea, a welcome change from the ubiquitous big white ones. Puddings didn't get a look in.

ADDRESS The Cut, London SE1 (020 7928 7211)
OPEN 12.00–15.00, 17.30–23.30
UNDERGROUND Waterloo

Mulala

Handily placed opposite the wonderful Curzon Mayfair cinema, Mulala at the Patio could be the basis for a great Saturday night if the right film was showing across the road, even though there are no clubs close by to finish off the evening, now that the Ace of Clubs has closed. It's the kind of place you could equally enjoy for a date, a birthday party or to bring your parents.

The Patio attracts a – great euphemisms of our time – 'more traditional' clientele during the week, though a surprisingly large number of them turned out to be interested in this Saturday evening affair which began in summer 1999, one year after the proprietors took over. Now Mulala has its own set of regulars, fairly evenly distributed across genders and age ranges. It's inexpensive for the area with starters at around £4 and mains from £8–£10, or you can sit in the bar for a drink.

Don't be put off by the fact that it's in a cellar; when you get downstairs you find Mulala smart but informal with the owners serving in their kitchen whites. The menu offers an imaginative range of modern European food unusually well done, and any restaurant which includes rabbit on the menu has my vote.

ADDRESS Patio, 16 Curzon Street, London W1 (020 7490 1889)
OPEN first Saturday of the month, from 20.00
MIX gay and lesbian
UNDERGROUND Green Park

The Peasant

On two floors of an old Victorian pub, The Peasant offers a menu that combines modern British with Pacific-Rim influences, with a Mediterranean mezze option available downstairs only. It's a gay-run place, but this is usually only ascertainable from the clientele in the evenings. The whole experience is well thought out, from the food to the unaccustomed pleasure of a full-length mirror in the restaurant toilet facing you while you pee.

The space downstairs retains some of the former pub's features: the large wooden bar, carved wooden ceiling and nineteenth-century mosaic floor. With its warm colours, low lighting and newspapers on hand it would be very easy to settle in here for an afternoon with a selection of mezze dishes and a couple of glasses of something red.

Room 240, the restaurant upstairs, opened in 1996, three years after The Peasant. This provides a rather more formal setting, brighter and more modern, with calming pale-green walls (to help the business lunches along, perhaps – the lunchtime clientele looks quite different from the usual evening crowd), crisp white table linen, stone sculptures displayed around the room, and good views of London. It's close to the old Ingersoll building and several old warehouses in the process of being converted into loft spaces.

The food is unfussy and usually very good. Menus are seasonally constructed – on a sharp autumn day a tower of sweet potato, tomato and mozzarella, followed by a soup plate of braised lamb and gooey polenta definitely hit the spot – and change regularly. Main courses come in at around £10; service is attentive without being too obtrusive. An unusual selection of beers takes equal billing with the wine list, and quite right too in a former pub. We should have sampled the pear cider, but a white-chocolate, prune and almond parfait proved more of a distraction

8.14

and then coffee and test-tube glasses of grappa sent us into orbit for the rest of the afternoon.

These two floors and the garden terrace seating 20 make this a perfect place for that les/gay occasion: the first date or the last. With plenty of space between the tables you can ogle or hiss at each other at your leisure without annoying anyone else – as if you'd either notice or care at either of those junctures.

ADDRESS 240 St John Street, London EC1 (020 7336 7726)
OPEN lunch, Monday to Friday, 12.30–15.00; dinner, Monday to Saturday, 18.30–23.00
UNDERGROUND Angel

eating

ther@py

On the basis that you go to 'Soho for bars, Mayfair for food' Elaine, proprietor of the Glass Bar (see page 4.22) has started this 'gay-friendly' restaurant, disbanding the clubs she used to run to devote herself to this new venture. ther@py is located in a development behind New Bond Street so new it wasn't in the A–Z yet, but easy to find (take the alley by the side of Cecil Gee). Lancaster Court looks as though it's aiming to recreate St Christopher's Place – a comparative oasis of calm behind the north side of Oxford Street and home to upmarket shops and restaurants.

ther@py has a leisurely quality to it, and a north African feel to the decor which on our visit was reflected in the menu, though this changes frequently and takes in Japanese, Middle Eastern and Modern European food. It's inexpensive considering that it's all organic – even the bottled water apparently – and there are set prices for one, two, or three courses or starters on their own, with plenty of vegetarian and vegan options. The gay-friendliness factor is probably more evident in the evenings, and its success is likely to depend on the word-of-mouth route, but the informal, friendly atmosphere will go a long way. Good food, cheaper than therapy, and you can drop into Armani or Versace on your way out if you want to complete the Bond Street experience.

ADDRESS 10–11 Lancaster Court, off New Bond Street, London W1
(020 7499 5554)
OPEN Monday to Friday, 12.00–15.00, Monday to Saturday,
19.00–22.00
MIX straight and gay
UNDERGROUND Bond Street

Vegetarian and Vegan Group

It's a common misconception that all lesbians are vegetarians. Does it come from the same people who think we have soft, cuddly-toy sex, and so wouldn't dream of eating a bunny wabbit? Is it that people assume lesbianism is a political choice that comes in the same package as animal rights and wearing comfortable shoes? Or is it that men = meat, and eschewing the one means not chewing the other? Wrong, wrong, wrong.

So prevalent is this attitude that I wondered why this group existed at all; lesbian meat-eaters may be a more beleaguered minority. The group, which started in 1997, was originally for men, but now also welcomes women because they don't want to exclude anyone, not even meat-eaters or straight people. Each month sees two events – visits to vegetarian restaurants (Ravi Shankar, a bhelpoori house in Euston; Veg, a vegan Chinese in Kensington; Manna in Hampstead) – walks, picnics or marches.

Dinner-table conversation is, surprise, about food: the odd confession of meat-eating, debates on the relative merits of soya chunks, Quorn and tofu. But the social aspects – meeting new people, making friends, cruising – which must be at least part of what draws people to the group were strangely absent. They were anxious to quash rumours that they dress up as vegetables for Pride. (Why not? It might be fun.) And no one seemed to be enjoying their food very much.

Each table took great pains to keep written accounts of everyone's order to facilitate bill-paying at the end. Well, it was something to talk about. We forgot to pay for our tea and when we remembered the next day we imagined some might say it was a deliberate act of sabotage.

ADDRESS c/o GVV, BM Box 5700, London WC1
OPEN twice monthly on Sunday
MIX lesbian and gay

eating

shopping

Books

Chains such as Borders, Books Etc and Waterstone's often have sizeable gay sections, especially the Charing Cross Road branches, presumably to cater for the nearby Compton Street market. These shops usually stock magazines and papers alongside books and are good for basic mainstream titles. Larger branches of chains are likely to have cafés where you can sit around and read books you have no intention of buying. No indication yet that any of these have been marked out as cruising grounds for particular sections of our community. It can only be a matter of time. Lesbian sections are often poor, try a visit to one of the shops listed below.

GAY'S THE WORD

Gay's The Word is London's only lesbian and gay bookstore, set up in 1979 for love not money – it's a non-profit-making venture. Originally much of the stock had to be imported, but this has changed considerably. The shop survived a charge of importing obscene materials after a raid in 1984 by HM Customs. Customers and authors supported the Defend Gay's The Word campaign; eventually the charges were withdrawn.

The shop seems tiny, an impression exaggerated by its narrowness, but manages to feel uncluttered despite its huge selection of books, videos, postcards, gay ephemera, badges. Specialist sections include antiquarian and second-hand books, lesbian and gay parenting and TV/TS.

Gay's The Word is a peaceful shop to linger in for an hour or so. GTW also hosts occasional evening readings and author events.

ADDRESS 66 Marchmont Street, London WC1 (020 7278 7654)
WEBSITE www.gaystheword.co.uk
OPEN Monday to Saturday, 10.00–18.30; Sunday, 14.00–18.00
UNDERGROUND Russell Square

Books

CENTERPRISE

Centerprise is a community centre in downtown Hackney and its bookshop has a definite neighbourhood feel. There's a small, well-chosen les/gay selection (as there should be, considering the location). Alongside the general fiction are black fiction and non-fiction, local history – some of which comes from Centerprise's writing workshops – and magazines (les/gay, ecology, art, politics). Centerprise also hosts readings and book launches and publishes *Calabash*, the black writers' journal.

ADDRESS 136–38 Kingsland High Street, London E8 (020 7254 9632)
OPEN Monday to Friday, 9.30–18.00; Saturday, 10.00–17.30;
Sunday, 14.00–18.00
BR Dalston Kingsland BUS 67, 76, 149, 236, 243

SILVER MOON

Silver Moon is the largest women's bookshop in Europe, has probably the most extensive lesbian selection in the UK, and is publisher of the popular lesbian detective-fiction series. So this is the place to come then.

Yes and no. The space itself causes a few problems: Silver Moon occupies three adjoining shops which are not as imaginatively amalgamated as they might have been. This means that despite the extensive stock this is not always the best place to browse – not least because of the narrow aisles. The space downstairs, which includes the lesbian section, noticeboard and free papers, feels more open, if still a little hushed.

ADDRESS 64–68 Charing Cross Road London WC2 (020 7836 7906)
OPEN Monday to Friday 9.30–17.30; Saturday, 10.00–18.30; Sunday, 12.00–18.00
UNDERGROUND Leicester Square

Home

Despite popular opinion, as immortalised in the second-date joke,* lesbians are no more or less obsessive about setting up home together than anyone else. But the nesting instinct does seem to be part of the deal. It goes like this: get the girlfriend, the joint mortgage, the incompatible pets, then bring on the homestore catalogues, learn to negotiate over paint colours and ignore her worrying attachment to dried flowers.

London is awash with design shops specialising in items for all parts of your home: these are only some of the most obvious choices. But whether you go to Conran or Argos, don't forget that you always knew it would end in tears.

HABITAT

Derided by style snobs but much frequented, Habitat now has a café attached. Predictably it's a Mediterranean café, with an attractive menu, but surrounded by the buzz of the shop it may not be the most relaxing place to discuss bathroom fittings. It's a far cry from the secluded hum of the Heal's restaurant next door, tucked behind the sofa department.

Many a lesbian couple can be seen in Habitat clutching a list and trying not to argue over the crockery. Here you can buy most items you need for your home, but beware Habitat's tendency to champion cooking utensils which turn out to be a flash in the, um, pan. Like that hot-rock cooker she bought for your last anniversary present.

ADDRESS 196 Tottenham Court Road, London W1 (020 7631 3880)
OPEN Monday to Wednesday, 10.00–18.00; Thursday, 10.00–19.00; Friday and Saturday, 9.00–18.30; Sunday, 12.00–18.00
UNDERGROUND Goodge Street/Warren Street

* Just in case someone, somewhere, hasn't heard it: Q: What does a lesbian bring on the second date? A: A removal van.

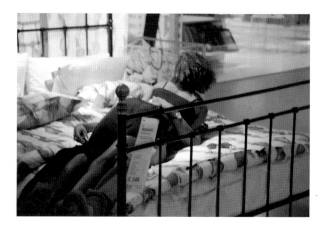

HEAL'S

Heal's shoppers come for stylish contemporary furniture (nothing strange or difficult), fittings and household kit. Here there is usually a higher proportion of gay men than lesbians and there are frequently stars to spot. I was once waiting to pay for something that fitted easily in a wire basket while Dawn French organised the entire male staff to carry her purchases to her car. But if you can disregard the scope for financial humiliation and advanced envy it's a wonderful shop. The staircase alone makes it worth a visit. And the sales are good.

The King's Road store is much smaller and lacks the muffled luxury of the departments upstairs in Tottenham Court Road. The interior and its contents don't quite live up to the glass frontage.

ADDRESS 196 Tottenham Court Road, London w1 (020 7636 1666), and 234 Kings Road, London sw3 (020 7349 8411)

OPEN Monday to Wednesday, 10.00–18.00; Thursday, 10.00–20.00; Friday, 10.00–18.30; Saturday, 9.30–18.30; Sunday 12.00–18.00

UNDERGROUND Goodge Street/Warren Street; Sloane Square

JOHN LEWIS

Not marketed as a style leader, though it keeps its end up well enough, the wonderfully comprehensive kitchen/household department at John Lewis covers everything from white goods to poultry lacers. It includes all the makes essential to the modern consumerist household – Dyson, Smeg, Miele, Dualit – and is 'never knowingly undersold' into the bargain. I overheard one assistant explaining that while one vacuum cleaner only picked up big crumbs, the other reached deep down. Perhaps the helpfulness of the staff, always on hand to ease you into your purchases, large or small, derives from the John Lewis Partnership's

employment practices, of a benevolent-capitalist persuasuion. If household isn't for you, you might try the fabrics department (big with gay men), linens or underwear (see page 9.20).

ADDRESS Oxford Street, London W1 (020 7629 7711)

OPEN Monday to Wednesday, 9.30–18.00; Thursday, 10.00–20.00; Saturday 9.00–18.00

UNDERGROUND Oxford Circus

IKEA

Tthe shop that has furnished thousands of lesbian homes – or if not, what are they all doing here? Try not to go at the weekend as it can get unbearably crowded. IKEA has a good reputation for its attention to customer services such as crèche facilities which are standard, as are child-sized tables for mini-diners, but checking on stock availability and delivery can be a nightmare. Upstairs is furniture and room set-ups, always a mixed bag. Downstairs is the marketplace, unstylishly laid out, but who cares?

In addition to the in-store restaurant – reindeer meat was more exciting for novelty value than taste – there is a food shop and take-out counter just beyond the tills. You may need to bolster your sugar levels at this point, depleted from exhaustion and wallet shock. You can drown your sorrows in Swedish airport fare: gravadlax, crispbreads, aquavit, and, incomprehensibly, Dime bars.

ADDRESS Neasden: 2 Drury Way, London NW10; Thurrock: Heron Way, West Thurrock, Essex (020 8208 5600 for all stores)

OPEN Monday to Friday, 10.00–20.00; Saturday and bank holidays, 10.00–18.00; Sunday, 11.00–17.00

UNDERGROUND Neasden then a 15-minute walk; BR Chalford Hundred

ROAD Neasden: A406 North Circular; Thurrock: M25, junctions 30/31

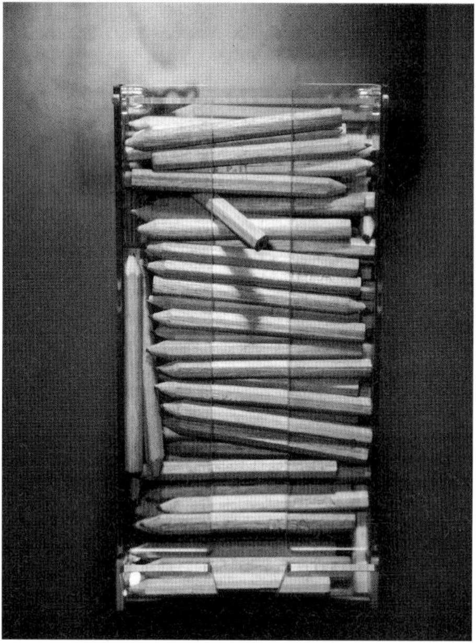

MAC

You may find all the lipstick-lesbian shtick overplayed and out of date, but if you want to wear make-up the question remains: where do you go for the means to a well-dressed face? Are you a Space nk-nik or a Boots girl, a slave to the Clarins counter or a devotee of Body Shop? Lips by Rimmel or Ruby and Millie?

Make-up and skincare products are accompanied by terminology that only Real Women with the patience for in-depth study can decipher. If you're not of that particular sisterhood, a prime consideration may be to avoid the scary, flawlessly made-up assistants who make the less sophisticated (me) feel of indeterminate gender – though the amount of slap they wear would put most trannies to shame. So the options are either to choose your brand carefully – a series of makeovers could do the trick if you've got the stamina – or to go for the self-service option.

How long does it take one lesbian to use six lipsticks? I don't know either, but you get a free one at mac if you take back six empties. mac's use of 'faces' RuPaul and kd lang indicates a healthy disrespect for so-called Real Women, and its assistants will guide you patiently through the range of colours and textures and offer tissues, make-up remover and helpful comments until, finally, 'that looks really good' and you depart with a new slim black toy. And if you go for brands with conscience, profits from their Viva Glam lipstick – once a favourite of Madonna's – go towards Aids research.

ADDRESS 28 Fouberts Place, London W1 (020 7534 9222) and branches
OPEN Monday to Saturday, 10.00–18.30
UNDERGROUND Oxford Circus

Otto

Otto optician's stands out on drab Highbury Corner, a bright warm box in red, orange and yellow underneath its four-eyes logo – OttO – or is it an emoticon, an internet symbol? A prominent rainbow flag in the window brings in more business than Yellow Pages, apparently Otto estimates that around 20 per cent of their customers are lesbian/gay, a high proportion even given its Islington location. Otherwise it's the usual round of passers-by wandering in for eye tests or to get their glasses repaired – a friendly optician has to rank as the fifth emergency service.

Alongside the demise of free nhs eye tests and the rise of customer-service culture, new technology involved has led to much higher expectations of opticians. Gone are the days of collecting your glasses so long after you chose them that you can barely remember what they looked like. Otto invested in a state of the art lens-cutting machine that saves both time and improves quality. And a small but stylish display of frames has a huge advantage over its competitors: all prices quoted include basic lenses, so you get a realistic idea of what your glasses are going to cost.

Glasses have never been an entirely convincing fashion item, despite recent geeky/speccy fashion – and Otto confirms that for most customers they are a grudge buy rather than a treat, health-related if chic. Still, Dorothy Parker may have been right about men, but girls do make passes at girls who wear glasses.

ADDRESS 15 Highbury Corner, London N5 (020 7700 7557)
OPEN Monday, Wednesday to Saturday, 10.30–18.30; Tuesday, 10.30–19.00
UNDERGROUND Highbury & Islington

Sex

SH!

If you're shopping for sex toys or fetish gear, Sh!, the 'women's erotic emporium', would be the most obvious destination. Proprietor Ky Hoyle has created a friendly, relaxed atmosphere designed to remove embarrassment – sex shops do have the capacity to reduce even the most grown up among us to sniggering teenagers. Men are allowed to shop there too, as long as women customers don't object. Browsing is encouraged and advice and cups of tea are freely given, but that doesn't mean you're forced to have intimate chats about your sexual habits.

On the ground floor you can find everything from 'starter packs' with dildo, lube and condoms to various weights of chain by the metre. There are leather and rubber goods – clothes, whips, crops, collars, harnesses, handcuffs, corsets, restraints, stockings and gloves – a forest of dildos ('representational and non-representational') and vibrators, nipple clamps and safer-sex paraphernalia: dental dams, gloves and condoms. The books and magazines include a good sexual-health section and then there is the inevitable selection of 'naughty novelties' such as After Dinner Nipples (mint crisps) and Lewdo.

Sh!'s catalogue (there's a full mail-order service) includes a booklet providing both descriptions of the merchandise for the uninitiated and sex tips.

ADDRESS 39 Coronet Street, London N1 6RT (020 7613 5458)
OPEN Monday to Saturday, 11.30–18.30; late night until 20.00 on Thursday; Sunday, 11.00–17.00
ACCESS ring the bell
UNDERGROUND Old Street
www.sh-womenstore.com

Ann Summers is the Superdrug of sex shops, complete with plastic baskets to emphasise that this is only shopping. The anonymous supermarket approach will suit some people, but it doesn't exactly up the erotic ante. The company has been in the market since 1973 (Sh!, by contrast, opened in 1992) but it still gives off that image of saucy underwear parties, and the forbidden-fruit logo (an apple with a bite taken out of it) accentuates this. Ann Summers describes itself as 'by women, for women', but it's a view of female sexuality of pensionable age, and one to bring a pro-sex 1990s woman out in hives. Redressing the balance in the sex industry it may be (it's a female-run company with gross annual turnover of £38 million) but this is an object lesson in the art of de-eroticisation. Yet it sells.

At the front of the flagship Charing Cross Road shop is tame underwear, PVC and lace basques and hot pants, and condoms. Only the range of lubes suggests anything more. At the entrance to the back room, the licenced sex shop, are two slightly askew mannequins looking like rejects from Selfridges: a Madame with a whip and a Tarzan in funfur leopardskin. This interesting couple sets the tone for a range of rubber and leatherware and appendages and appliances in cellophane packages with diagrams and instructions for use, so you don't need to ask; lots of soft-core straight porn; Monstercock, 'just like the real thing'; Dick Tasty rub-on; and, best of all, Toy of Joy, a vibrating vagina with pubic hair.

ADDRESS main branch: 155 Charing Cross Road, London WC1 (020 7437 1886)
OPEN Monday to Saturday, 10.00–20.45; Sunday, 12.00–19.45
UNDERGROUND Tottenham Court Road

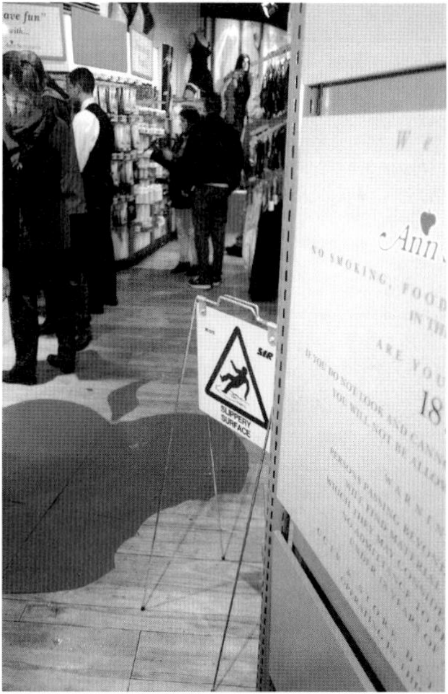
SLIPPERY
SURFACE
NO SMOKING,
ARE YOU
18

Underwear

Who is responsible for the cheesy remark that the sign of a woman in love is buying new underwear? In, out or pending, where to buy knickers is an important business. Gay branding may have pushed Calvin Kleins into an unassailable position, along with Jockey and Sloggi, but here are some other options, probably in a high street near you.

MARKS & SPENCER
M&S is famous both for standard dyke-issue cotton knickers, in an array of cuts and colours, and as housing 'the temple of silk at Marble Arch' (in the hugest M&S in the country) for the serious femme. It also sells one or two other useful items – try the foodhall.
ADDRESS main branch: 458 Oxford Street, London W1 (020 7935 7954)
OPEN Monday to Friday, 9.00–20.00; Saturday, 9.00–19.00; Sunday 12.00–18.00
UNDERGROUND Marble Arch

MUJI
A visit to Japanese temple of minimalism Muji will get you its brand of non-branded but highly recognisable neutral-coloured, ribbed, combed-cotton knickers and a matching pack of three essential vests for all seasons.
ADDRESS 26 Great Marlborough Street, London W1 (020 7494 1197), and branches
OPEN Monday to Wednesday, Saturday, 10.00–18.30; Thursday, 10.00–19.00; Sunday, 12.00–18.00
UNDERGROUND Oxford Circus

AGENT PROVOCATEUR
Agent Provocateur in Soho, which looks like a sex shop from the street, is the current destination of choice for designer girly underwear in fantastic fabrics and colours for those with well-endowed wallets. It also does a line in diamanté collars and prettified fetish jewellery.
ADDRESS 6 Broadwick Street, London W1 (020 7439 0229)
OPEN Monday to Saturday, 11.00–19.00
UNDERGROUND Oxford Circus

JOHN LEWIS
If you suspect you might be a member of the national majority whose bras don't fit you couldn't do better than John Lewis in Oxford Street. The lingerie department offers a measuring service second to none. Matronly women measure you up and then reappear with suitable alternatives according to your needs and bank balance. And they manage to fit you up perfectly without ever mentioning the part of your anatomy you are attempting to clothe: 'Lift yourself into the cup dear.' But maybe 'yourself' is a euphemism to distract attention from the fact that all the assistants have the original shelf-like chests that no amount of uplifting and enhancing is going to give me. Still, it's the kindness you would expect at John Lewis.
ADDRESS Oxford Street, London W1 (020 7629 7711)
OPEN Monday to Wednesday, 9.30–18.00; Thursday, 10.00–20.00; Saturday, 9.00–18.00
UNDERGROUND Oxford Circus

Columbia Road Flower Market

'Daisy, Daisy, give me your answer, do,
I'm half crazy all for the love of you …'

A Sunday-morning *passegiata* for the partnered and currently uncoupled of all sexual persuasions, Columbia Road is a social space to meet and greet old friends and to spy potential new interests – you can stalk her around the stalls and, with luck and good judgement, contrive a meeting at one of the cafés. Food opportunities include cakes, a fish shop for tubs of calamari and tiger prawns along with whelks and jellied eels, kippers at Jones' café and bagels (but make sure you don't get caught mid-bagel by the woman of your dreams). You might even have time to buy some flowers.

There's always a smattering of gay men in night-scented and indoor varieties: those for whom Saturday night is not yet over, the visit to the market being another post-club stop, and those anxiously inspecting trellises and wondering whether a berberis or a ceanothus is the right buy.

Many of the shops – garden furniture, hats, essential oils, clothes, kitchenware, jewellery – are open only on market day. (The market is limited in size and opening hours by planning regulations and it's quite deserted the rest of the week.) It's less crowded the earlier you go, but if you're not overly claustrophobic the best bargains are to be had during the last hour. The Royal Oak pub on the corner is gay and is often used in film shoots as an 'authentic East End boozer'.

ADDRESS Columbia Road, London E2
OPEN weekly on Sunday, 8.00–13.00
BUS 8, 26, 55, 67, 149, 243

Portobello Road Market

There can't be too many streets in London where dykes, Trustafarians, debs and tourists all share the same pavement. Portobello Road is really several markets that co-exist quite happily. A walk the length of the street from Notting Hill to the Westway takes you first past the collectors' antiques market, mainly furniture and jewellery – dealers arrive here from 4.00. You pass through a section that seems to specialise in old cameras and etchings, near the old Electric Cinema (always about to reopen, never does), and after you cross Elgin Crescent you're in a fruit and veg market, with the occasional olive and chilli stall, until you reach the far end with its stalls of army-surplus and new clothes, dodgy socks and posters.

Portobello Green under the flyover has suffered the fate that befalls so many market areas, where indoor fixed pitches or niche shoplets threaten to turn the whole area into an upmarket gift mall. There's no indication anywhere that this is the home of the annual August bank-holiday Notting Hill Carnival apart from a couple of record shops and a few drummers.

It sounds like a long walk and it is, but refreshment is never far away: highlights include the Malaysian restaurant by the Westway and the Spanish supermarket. And there are some sights to see, like a barrel-organ grinder with minature dogs in an antique pram. It wasn't clear what he was selling, but the RSPCA should probably be told.

ADDRESS Portobello Road, London W10 and W11
OPEN mainly on Friday and Saturday
UNDERGROUND Notting Hill Gate

Spitalfields Market

Spitalfields is one of the markets on the edge of the City which together create an almost continuous swathe (the others are Brick Lane and Petticoat Lane). Situated between Bethnal Green and Liverpool Street, it most obviously straddles the rich City/poor East End division of the area. It's surrounded by 'loft developments' and its future has at times been uncertain, with developers circling over the prime site, since the fruit and vegetable market moved out in the 1980s.

Shops opening on to both street and market sides selling hats, organic food, flowers, contemporary furniture and useless items in fluorescent plastic (all the usual stuff you might covet or be bored stupid by) form a border to the market stalls. These include an extensive and very good organic-food section, coffee, bakery, olive and tofu stalls, a charcuterie shop (some meat, phew), clothes, collectable tat, records and tapes, candles, bags and furniture. For eat-now food there's falafels, burritos, pasta, stir-frys, crêpes and curries. At the far end are the sports pitches, and artists exhibiting work in a permanent open studio. The tenants of the artists' studios on the Liverpool Street side were evicted in 1998, on one of the occasions when the market was under threat of redevelopment. Glad though I am that this threat has been lifted for now, it seems a little sad that Spitalfields has only managed to secure its future by feeding Londoners' apparently limitless appetite for shopping. Still, long may it remain between developments, and while it does, it's worth a visit.

ADDRESS Commercial Street, London E1
OPEN weekly on Sunday
UNDERGROUND Liverpool Street

health and fitness

Basketball

Basketball is quite a new sport for lesbians in this country and the London Cruisers were the only UK gay team at the Amsterdam Gay Games in 1998. The Cruisers clearly have a friendly set-up, designed to be very open to new players and beginners with one of their two weekly practices being a coaching session. Thursday night is more of a fitness session and constant bouncing: practising shooting on the run, passing, blocking and marking, set moves, talking tactics. They don't play in any league, it's friendlies only with local teams.

As ever, the clothes are good, the camaraderie ready. The tattoo of bouncing balls is faintly hypnotic so that when it finally stops it's quite shocking. Ever the non-participant on these occasions, I think basketball is a great sport to watch and despite my memory throwing up images of gigantic Harlem Globetrotters, height doesn't seem to be an indicator of success. Though it can't hurt.

Maybe by the time their two teams go to Zürich for the next Gay Games in 2000, basketball will have become the new volleyball. Anyone with hoop dreams should go and play, and I would too if I could learn to catch.

ADDRESS Bethnal Green Performing Arts Centre, Gossett Road, London E2 (020 7372 4385 for London Cruisers organiser)
PRACTICE Thursday, 19.30–21.00 (women-only), and Sunday afternoons (mixed)
ACCESS £5 weekly membership, open

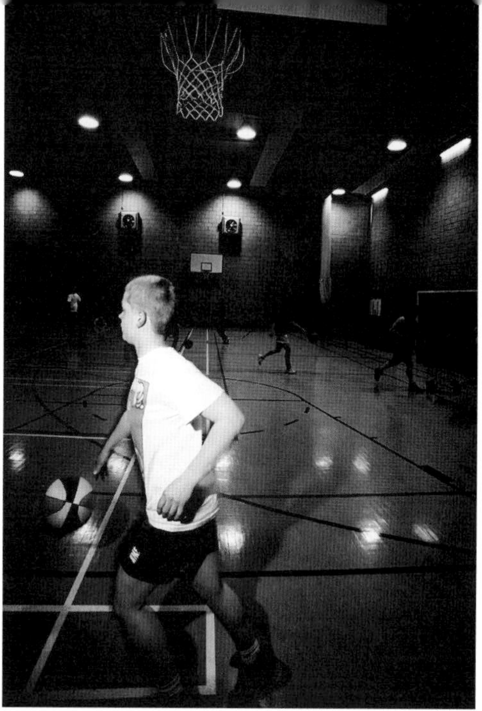

Bernhard Clinic

'There's no way to make this entirely pleasant,' the nurse said as I lay, legs in stirrups, waiting for an internal examination. I couldn't agree more, but the Bernhard experience – a sexual-health service for lesbians – is probably as good as it gets. It takes a little getting used to the strange openness in the surgery about sexual practice, the blessed absence of questions about contraception, the ease of discussion about sexual history, the explanations accompanying each step of the process, the conversation about incidence of cervical cancer and digital transmission.

And it's not just (almost) pleasant, it's very thorough. Alongside the screening for stds (results while you wait), safer-sex information and free latex gloves, condoms and lube on offer are demonstrations of breast-examination techniques, hiv testing on request (results given only in person, always accompanied by testing for hepatitis). Testing for syphilis, which is alarmingly on the increase, is part of the service.

If Hammersmith is inconvenient, you could try the Audre Lorde clinic at the Royal London in Whitechapel, which offers a similar service; the two clinics may be involved in joint projects in the future in this under-researched field. An added attraction to this feast of reason is that appointments are easy to come by and organised so you don't waste hours in the waiting room.

ADDRESS Department of GU Medicine, Charing Cross Hospital, Fulham Palace Road, London W6 (020 8846 1576/1577)
OPEN weekly on Wednesday, 16.00–19.00
UNDERGROUND Hammersmith/Barons Court
BUSES 11, 220, 295

Brixton Rec

The smell of plimsolls and sports surfaces greets you. The second impression is that there are too many stairs up from street level and then escalators up to pool level. But once you're in the pool area, after marvelling at the size, cleanliness and innovative features of the changing rooms, it all makes sense. It's a big broad pool and the bonus of it being on the first floor is that you can look at the sky as you swim and watch trains going past, over the arches of Brixton market. If you're doing backstroke, the wooden ceiling is equally pleasant to look at, with lateral glazing bringing in a good deal of light. That's plenty to keep you occupied while you get your lengths in. The main pool is joined to the training pool by a tributary channel, and one level up you can see poor deluded souls working out in the gym. Women-only sessions are three times per week, possibly to accommodate all the lesbians here, in singles, couples, groups and families.

Aside from the pool and gym facilities, the Rec has all the usual racquet sports, cricket and bowls, a climbing wall and a sports bar (with a big-screen TV) to slob out in afterwards.

ADDRESS 27 Brixton Station Road, London SW9 (020 7926 9779)
OPEN Monday to Friday, 7.00–23.00; Saturday and Sunday, 8.00–20.00
ACCESS depends on activity
UNDERGROUND Brixton

Football

Should you be loitering by the bagel shop in Ridley Road market at midday on Sunday during the football season, you might notice a group of dykes congregated outside. Hardly unusual in Hackney, you might think, though it's not the most obvious place to hang out. It's the Hackney Women's Football Club meeting to go to an away match.

There are around 30 in the squad and in the team's eight years of existence it has reached the dizzy heights of the second division of the Greater London Premier League, but hasn't won anything yet: 'Don't be silly.' Sack the manager, I say.

The reason trotted out for the lack of press coverage of women's football is that it's a participative not a spectator sport – and on a cold December afternoon, this team could certainly have used a few more supporters. As it was, some of them sloped off at half-time to watch the Arsenal match in the pub, naturally the centre of off-pitch activity for footballers, whatever their sexuality or gender. The team only scored once, so there wasn't much chance to check out the post-goal snog-fest so common on the small screen … though it looked a little low key.

There are other teams in all parts of London, and if this sounds a little serious it shouldn't be too difficult to find one which takes a less hard-line approach, like the old Fag and Bottle squad which played in both north and south London.

ADDRESS home matches, Mabley Green, Homerton Road, London E9; practices Britannia Leisure Centre, 40 Hyde Road, London N1
OPEN matches on Sunday afternoon, 14.00; practices weekly on Wednesday, 18.00–21.00, on floodlit pitches next to Britannia
MIX women-only
BUS Mabley Green 236, S2; Britannia Leisure Centre 76, 141

GLUG

No, it's nothing to do with drinking. It stands for Gay and Lesbian Underwater Group and it's for scuba divers. It's a national organisation with around 70 members and a satellite group in Bristol. Around 20 per cent of the membership are women and numbers are apparently rising. Every year some 40 trips are organised around the UK coastline – including eco-activities like beach cleaning – and worldwide, including, in the recent past, Cambodia, Curacao (for Diving for Life, the Ninth International Gay and Lesbian Diving Jamboree), France and the Solomon Islands. At the UK Gay Olympics in July 2000 GLUG were offering try-dives to participants and supporters, and if you haven't tried it before, it's a good way to start.

It's a group for experienced divers rather than beginners; you need to have your PADI (Professional Association of Diving Instructors) qualification under your wetsuit to be a real member. To this end GLUG can advise you on good places to go to get the qualification.

The group used to meet at Central Station in King's Cross, a venue as far from clear blue seas as you could imagine; now they have moved to the Old Quebec near Marble Arch, no nearer the coast and no more environmentally welcoming. I was the sole female at the meeting I attended; I was made very welcome, my opinion was solicited at every turn and I said I'd be back in touch when I'd got my PADI.

ADDRESS The Quebec, Old Quebec Street, London W1
(020 7625 5789, before 21.30)
OPEN monthly on first Tuesday, 20.00
MIX lesbian and gay
UNDERGROUND Marble Arch

Ironmonger Row Baths

A prime example of 1930s municipal architecture, housing two pools, a gym, a health suite and a laundry with an enormous pressing machine that looks as though it would iron your clothes into oblivion.

Everybody says that swimming pools are heaving with lesbians – those interested in a little light toning-up but too weedy or lazy to expose themselves in a gym. It may be so, but 'everybody' is obviously not as short-sighted as I am. What may for others be an opportunity to admire a well-turned thigh executing perfect breaststroke passes by in a relaxing blur. So I can't comment, even though I use it often, except to say that it's rarely crowded and I especially like the building.

The gym looks over the main pool so you can work out and watch the bathing belles doing their stuff. On Wednesday and Friday evenings there's an acquarobics class in the shallow pool – I swear I've heard them robicing to 'We Are Family' (regular mix), but it sounds like fun anyway.

Downstairs is the health suite, where the high level of lesbian clientele makes for quality overheard conversations. Early arrivals occupy the daybeds – recessed into wooden surrounds, survivors from the original fittings. A refurbishment in the mid-1990s added more – but never enough – lounger seats to go with the dry- and wet-heat rooms, the plunge pool, the smoking room and the rub-down area. Shiatsu this is not, but it certainly gets rid of dead skin so you emerge freshly scrubbed if no more healthy.

ADDRESS Ironmonger Row, London EC1 (020 7253 4011)
OPEN swimming, Monday to Thursday, 6.30–21.30; Friday, 7.30–19.00; Turkish bath, Monday, 14.00–21.30; Wednesday, Friday, 9.00–21.30; Sunday, 10.00–18.30
ACCESS depends on activity
UNDERGROUND Old Street

PUBLIC BATHS
& WASH HOUSES

health and fitness

Jubilee Hall

Aside from being a charitable sports trust with one of the best selections of free weights in central London, Jubilee Hall has an interesting 20-year history of providing sports and fitness facilities in Covent Garden. Built at the turn of the century, it was originally designed as a market hall for cut flowers. When the Covent Garden market moved in 1978, local people squatted the building (and played five-a-side football matches there) in protest against demolition plans, eventually managing to get the hall listed and then developed into the mixed-use space it is now.

It is this history that underpins the ethos of the club: market rates for membership but hefty discounts for unemployed and disabled people, kids' clubs and charitable work. And it's a very visible history too, as you look out over the rest of the market from the vaulted gym. There's space for badminton, basketball, volleyball and five-a-side football; martial arts and dance classes and complementary-medicine sessions. All new members get a free gym induction and training programme and there are personal trainers for an extra fee.

Anyone can walk in and use the gym for £6.90 or attend a class for £6.00 without a membership. While this isn't a gay gym, there are significant numbers of gay staff and members.

On our visit I was amazed at how many people must have got up and come straight in for a work-out – and I noticed that the café, with an interesting menu featuring Maltesers and protein shakes, smelled of bacon.

ADDRESS 30 The Piazza, London WC2 (020 7836 4007/4835)
OPEN Monday to Friday, 7.00–22.00; Saturday, 10.00–18.00; Sunday, 10.00–17.00
ACCESS call for membership details/class costs
UNDERGROUND Covent Garden

health and fitness

Porchester Hall

Porchester Hall did not want to be featured in this guide. No, we couldn't take photographs, not even when it was empty; no, they only allowed a certain number of journalists in each year; no, there was no marketing manager in post at the moment; no, she hadn't got the fax because the machine was on the other side of the building; and what was the book about again?

Ms Homophobe aside, this beautiful local-authority bath house built in 1926 is a delight, boasting dry- and wet-heat rooms, plunge and swimming pools, a jacuzzi, beauty-treatment rooms and a domed rest room upstairs, for women of all persuasions.

Having paid your money you're bombarded by notices exhorting you to turn off your mobile and not use the place as an office (now there's an idea). As you enter the lower sanctum another notice pleads for quiet conversations. Yet another advises of the times when schmeissing is permitted, whatever that means.

If it's not too busy you can mark your territory – a couch – with your gingham wrap, included in the price along with the two disappointingly small towels. You can hear the lapping of the pool as someone dares to plunge. And you should too: overcome the fear of a heart attack. Until 20.00 the price includes a swim and even a couple of lengths can make you feel virtuous. Add this to a fearless, invigorating dip in very cold water and it's almost a night of exercise, what with the severe pummelling your muscles take in the jacuzzi.

After all that exertion you need to indulge in some languid slothing and concentrate on sloughing off the week along with the dead skin. The subdued lighting in the upstairs space is restful; women chat (quietly of course), read (overhead light if needed), sleep, smoke, anoint themselves, wander around naked with facemasks on. There's a small menu: tea and

toasted sandwiches, salads, jacket potatoes – but beware, it's easy to miss last orders.

After a few rounds of the facilities, a power shower is the last stop before copious moisturiser. You'll leave feeling blissed out, cleansed and set up for the weekend.

ADDRESS Porchester Road, London W2 (020 7792 3980)
OPEN Tuesday, Thursday and Friday, 10.00–22.00, last
entry 20.00; Sunday, 10.00–16.00, last entry 14.00;
MIX women-only
ACCESS £18.70 non-members; annual membership £37.40, then £13.65
each visit
UNDERGROUND Bayswater

Softball

A group of women in Clissold Park between April and September pitching and catching in different formations can only mean one thing. It's the Hackney Handbags softball team on a Saturday afternoon practice. Softball has long been a dyke favourite – check the press to find a team near you – and there are mixed gay teams in London as well.

'Don't call it rounders', I was warned after an early slip-up. I'll have to say instead that it's not a million miles away from baseball so fans of Madonna in *A League of Their Own* won't be disappointed, but happily the Handbags don't go in for 1940s fashion. To enjoy yourself at softball you need to be able to catch and wield a big bat (check out that nice action), and you get to wear a baseball-like glove so that catching the ball becomes a possibility instead of something you'd run a mile from. A sharp clang of ball on metal replaces the chock of leather on willow of the cricket pitch.

Incapable of hitting balls with bats, I wasn't about to join in, although beginners are welcome and training is geared to individual need. Part of the practice involved a game and there was much encouragement and general whooping going on. And it's then that you realise how many softball-related phrases have crept into everyday language: three strikes and you're out, I'll swing for her, pitching ideas, stuck at first base, home free … Linguistics aside, I can report that for the sports-challenged it's a good game to watch. For some of us it's enough risk taking to sit within injury distance of the ball.

ADDRESS practices and home games Clissold Park, Stoke Newington Church Street, London N16 (0958 388021)
OPEN practice, Saturday morning; matches, weekday evenings/weekends
MIX women only
ACCESS £35 per year (to cover insurance etc)

The Women's Gym

Gym culture exploded during the 1980s and it's generally a very commercial and competitive scene: if you want to get fit you have to pay for it and you have to look the part as well. The Women's Gym, an independent space at the Sobell Centre, started in 1983 and operates very differently. For a start it's non-profit making, and targets women who have been put off using most gym facilities because of ability, age, size and low income. There's an enlightened membership policy with flexible concessionary rates, no punitive penalties for cancellation, and a free crèche at lunchtimes. And you won't be intimidated by a roomful of lithe bodies in Lycra.

Staff are trained to work with mixed-ability classes – a tall order in a limited space, but judging by the response one they're meeting. So as well as the usual multi-gym and free weights, circuit training and body conditioning, there are classes in yoga, gentle exercise, massage for women with disabilities and aromatherapy, a list that changes depending on demand.

There's a realistic attitude to keeping fit: together with Hammersmith Hospital, The Women's Gym has received funding for a study into the relationship between body fat and exercise, or, as they put it, to find out what's the least exercise you can get away with. Which is what we all want to know.

ADDRESS Sobell Leisure Centre, Hornsey Road, London N7
(020 7700 1141)
OPEN Monday to Friday, 9.00–22.30; Saturday, 9.00–18.00;
Sunday, 9.00–21.30
MIX women only
ACCESS prices vary
UNDERGROUND Finsbury Park

classes

Kickboxing

Without the benefit of sound it's hard to convey the full kickboxing experience as every punch has a noise, and you can hear the shouts as you come up Chenies Street towards the Drill Hall (see page 4.12) where the back-to-back classes at three stages are all very busy. At this level shouting itself might be enough to deter any potential attacker – classes are taught to use noise as a weapon to ward off attackers and to raise confidence. With that and the constant dancing on the spot *à la* Ali, kickboxing is clearly very empowering. As kickboxing is a self-defence discipline, the classes focus on how to use your skills responsibly.

It's also very good exercise. But kickboxing has a strong element of theatre to it as well: 'Come on, you're not being convincing enough,' berated the instructor Kelly when fearsome facial expressions and shouting fade. Classes may be short but she keeps them moving constantly, only quick water breaks being allowed.

In a rehearsal studio with mirrored walls much of the class is spent punching at your own reflection, or practicing ducking and moving out of range of your partner's punches – as much a part of kickboxing as hitting anyone. There's one strict instruction, often repeated: 'Please do NOT hit your partner', but for weedy onlookers, keeping close to the corner still seemed advisable.

ADDRESS 16 Chenies Street, London WC1 (020 7631 1353)
OPEN weekly on Monday, first class at 19.30
MIX women-only
UNDERGROUND Tottenham Court Road, Warren Street

Pink Singers

With an avowedly non-religious, non-racist and non-sexist approach to the repertoire, it's a wonder the Pink Singers can find anything to sing at all. But they've been managing for more than 15 years which makes them the longest-running lesbian and gay chorus in Europe.

Every Sunday around 35 people – a mix of newcomers to the scene and old lags – show up for rehearsals at the Drill Hall, drawn to the social side of the choir as well as to the singing. It's a non-auditioning choir and not only for the musically talented, though you have to be able to hold a tune. Members take whichever parts suit them best – men singing alto and women tenor raise no eyebrows here. Some people can't read music but they can take tapes home to practise with and there are workshops to improve skills. Their repertoire covers some of the obvious bases – Village People and Cole Porter as well as Brahms and their in-house composers. 'Happy Together', their anniversary tune, took the roof off at rehearsal.

Many of their performances take place at London Lighthouse, and they sing in Europe and the US too, raising the travel expenses through subscriptions. Some people were wearing Pink Singers t-shirts even at rehearsal – and sweetly, or so it seemed on this particular afternoon, they each carried their music in a pink ringbinder.

ADDRESS rehearsals at Drill Hall, 16 Chenies Street, London WC1 (020 7637 8270)
OPEN practice weekly on Sunday, 14.00
MIX lesbian and gay
ACCESS subscriptions £2 per rehearsal; annual membership £15/£5 unwaged
UNDERGROUND Goodge Street

Rubber Medusa's Bridge Club

At the end of one evening at the Bridge Club I had managed to play in two games of bridge – but with very little idea of what was going on, though I had worked out that a rubber is the term for winning two hands. Around 16 women is an average turnout, and though they're very keen – extra-curricular Saturday-night spin-off games are not unknown – most don't take it too seriously, you're not expected to turn up with a partner and beginners are made very welcome. There's lots of patient teaching and help on hand, but it's still mystifying, even when you can see the cards, and if you harbour ideas about getting into character and knocking back the hard stuff – pink gin, perhaps? – you'll have no chance. Laying the cards down is easy enough, it's the bidding that counts, and then remembering who's laid what and when.

Bridge, as you may have gathered, is a whole new (and suggestive) language: 'Is this your first time?', 'There comes a point where you have to stop' and so on. Forget Bridget Jones, a singleton means having only one card in a particular suit, then there's the auction and the contract. Playing bridge, I was assured, leads to other sorts of contracts. I bet.

ADDRESS basement of St George's Tavern, Hugh Street, London SW1 (020 7727 5379)
OPEN weekly on Tuesday, 19.30–23.00
MIX women-only
ACCESS £2
UNDERGROUND London Bridge/Borough

Yoga

In an airy top-floor space of a large building in fashionable Southwark, just up the road from Borough Market and the fish! restaurant and not far from Tate Modern, London's only lesbian yoga class takes place. It's the familiar white-painted yoga room with wooden floor and a few pillars, useful for support in certain yoga poses. But there the similarity with other classes ends. For a start there isn't the usual forbidding silence punctuated only with serious breathing and – shock – people can be heard to laugh.

Which isn't to suggest that this is a frivolous class, just that it's not intimidatingly serious, especially important for beginners. This would be a welcoming class whether you're immersing yourself in the practice, spiritual and physical, or just there to relax and stretch.

Although one of the purposes of yoga is to transcend the specifics of existence (race, class, sexuality …) a lesbian-only class is not viewed sympathetically by the establishment. Yoga is for everyone, runs the criticism, so why be divisive by having a lesbian-only class? It's a question that will have as many answers as respondants, depending on your attitudes to gender, sexuality, spirituality, and exercise, but there is clearly no shortage of takers.

ADDRESS The Yoga Space, Globe House, 2a Crucifix Lane, London Bridge, London SE1 (020 7378 1177)
OPEN Monday, 20.00–21.30
MIX women-only
ACCESS £6/£4
UNDERGROUND London Bridge

days out

Brighton

Brighton comes any way you want it: oyster and champagne bars or fish and chips on the (pebbly) beach; Regency villas in ice-cream shades or sink estates beyond the tourist drag. Traditionally the home of dirty weekends and dirty dealings, it has a long tradition of lesbian and gay residents and visitors, and as late as the mid-1980s was a warren of clubs for the pre-Pride homosexual. Now the red-plush palaces have disappeared and in the high-visibility 1990s Brighton became the gay mecca of the south coast, with clubs, shops, restaurants, B&Bs, tea shops, rollerblading – and the sea with the usual attractions such as jetskis and windsurfing and even, for major risk-takers, swimming.

Arrive by train and you can gasp at the sea view as you leave the station. It never gleams as blue as in 1960s Technicolor postcards – which you can still buy – but when the sun's out it still glints appealingly. A sunny day at the seaside has its charms, but Brighton's more atmospheric in the gloom: think *Brighton Rock* and *Mona Lisa*.

The seafront has recently undergone a California-style rebirth: you can get an open-air massage or a mehndi tattoo; nifty-footed extroverts can do ballroom dancing, tap, disco and line dancing surrounded by beachside bars, seafood restaurants and pot-of-tea-and-cake emporia. The West Pier, which set a standard for Victorian seaside architecture, is still a wreck, but a beautiful one and debates are raging about whether it should be refurbished. The Palace Pier, which may be renamed the Brighton Pier (giving a hint about the West Pier's future), offers all the usual pier tack.

Most of the antiques and second-hand clothes shops once worth visiting are either well plundered by now or absurdly expensive, but shopping is one of Brighton's pleasures still. Avoid the glitzy, touristy area of The Lanes and concentrate instead on The Parallels (the streets around

Kensington Street), a good shopping and hanging-out area. There are many new-age/personal-growth opportunities here – Hopi ear candle shops and the like. Not to mention Heavy Petting, for your gay pet products ('glitter for the glamour puss'). Brighton's that kind of place. Or for more regular shopping the full complement of chain stores awaits you in Western Road, leading to the more genteel Hove ('Hove, actually,' say residents when asked if they live in Brighton).

For afternoon tea – and afternoon tea is a must – the choice is huge, but the Mock Turtle (in Pool Valley, just off the seafront) is a long-standing favourite, offering such delights as Welsh rarebit, poached egg on toast and excellent home-made cakes, a change from cappuccino and carrot cake. Terre à Terre, another popular haunt, provides a changing menu of imaginative vegetarian food from snacks to multi-course extravaganzas. Brighton has always been well supplied with restaurants and pubs: for lesbian and gay venues check the press or ring Switchboard – the club Prickly Fish and the Shebeen bar are current favourites.

If you have to get out of the rain there are multiplexes with the usual fare, including one on the seafront, or if you go to Preston Circus (about 15 minutes up London Road) you'll find the Duke of Yorks, an independent repertory cinema. Another five minutes' walk brings you to Preston Park, a great sloping spread of green complete with rose garden and a café famous for egg and crinkly chips. This is where Pride is held. The ridiculous Pavilion, where *Richard III* was filmed, is worth a visit on a wet day. The Pavilion Gardens is a good place to lounge, eat ice cream and drink even more tea. The day I walked through a small orchestra was playing 'Over the Rainbow' – very Brighton somehow.

If you're staying for the weekend, the South Downs are close by for serious walking and that 'on top of the world ma' feeling. Devil's Dyke

Brighton

is a popular spot for obvious reasons. An hour's walk along the coast to the west brings you – via the Marina, monument to 1980s development – to Rottingdean, home of the twee tea shop. A car or bus will get you to Saltdean Lido, a stunning 1930s complex where you can still swim and lounge in summer.

TRAIN from Victoria or King's Cross Midland ROAD M25/M23, takes up to 2½ hours depending on which side of London you're driving from

Daytime Dykes

Daytime Dykes was set up in 1994 by the late Jackie Forster, famed lesbian feminist activist who, on reaching retirement age (though retired is not a word to be used about her), wondered where all the lesbians went during the day. Good question.

Twice a month, around 20 women meet to visit a museum or gallery, or, especially during the summer, for a (feminist) walk in central London. Venues are either cheap or free – essential given that a sizeable proportion of women are either retired or unemployed. All ages are welcome though the organisers do point out that it's not suitable for under-16s. There's no joining fee – a mere 50 pence is exacted for the kitty on each outing, anything left over going towards the summer picnic or Christmas party.

Daytime Dykes have been everywhere from the National Portrait Gallery to the Institute of Mechanical Engineers; the Army Museum and the Shri Swaminarayan Mandir Hindu temple in Neasden are among the favourites popular enough for a return visit. The programme features all the standard places as well as many less well-known, such as the St Barts Hospital Museum and the Mount Pleasant Postal Sorting Office Tour. Fishmongers Hall scored the highest turnout, a record-breaking 31; our visit to the Theatre Museum brought forth 29 women. Suggestions for future events are welcome.

When daytime turns into evening the group often retreats to a café or pub, where the shared visit makes for easy socialising.

PHONE 020 8673 6738
WEBSITE http://www.expage.com/page/daytimedykes
OPEN first and third Wednesday in the month
MIX women-only
ACCESS 50 pence per outing

Direct Line Insurance International Ladies Tennis Championships

This Eastbourne tournament is essentially a warm-up for Wimbledon, taking place in the preceding week. But don't think this means second class: weather permitting, you can see all the women players who count – Venus and Serena Williams, Novotna, Sanchez Vicario, Seles, Zvereva, Martinez – and take in some serious lesbian spotting as well.

Outside tennis, where else have lesbians been so visible? It's an honourable tradition: Billy Jean King, Martina Navratilova, plenty of probably slanderous changing-room gossip, even Rita Mae Brown as (centre) court scribe. More old-style butch dykes than the lineswomen you would be hard pressed to find outside archive photographs. Happy hours were spent peering at lesbians through the telephoto lens, when the photographer wasn't documenting the strange habit of stowing spare tennis balls in the leg of your knickers – probably the only occasion when public fiddling with your underwear is sanctioned. We thought of asking for an announcement: 'Would all lesbians please go to court number 2 for a group photograph.' We didn't need to bother. They were all there anyway.

The catering facilities hark back to a best-forgotten era of English history. Having sampled what was on offer, we understood why people came armed with Tupperware boxes and Thermos flasks, even if it meant having to picnic in uncertain early-summer weather.

So, altogether a good day out, even if you're less than fanatical about tennis, though football supporters – and every four years the tournament coincides with the World Cup – may find the crowd response a little tame.

OPEN week before Wimbledon (mid/late June)
ACCESS call 01323 72200 for ticket information
TRAIN to Eastbourne from Victoria

Direct Line Insurance International Ladies Tennis Championships

Sissinghurst Castle Gardens

A visit to the home and gardens of writer Vita Sackville-West – lover of Violet Trefusis and inspiration for Virginia Woolf's *Orlando* – and Harold Nicholson, is practically a lesbian pilgrimage. Vita and Harold's is probably England's most famous lavender marriage, described by their son Nigel Nicholson in *Portrait of a Marriage*, which was then made into a TV serial starring Janet McTeer as Vita, casting that created one lesbian icon playing another.

Vita died at Sissinghurst in 1962 and in 1967 the property became part of the National Trust. The volunteer NT staff don't know or don't tell about the unusual domestic arrangements, instead suggesting that Vita and Harold had studies in separate buildings – hers in the tower, his in the cottage – to enable them to concentrate on their work. Nor does sexuality feature in any of the guides on sale, except in the coyest terms: she is referred to as 'flamboyant' and 'a little wild' and mention is made of the 'turbulent years' of their marriage. But even given this revisionism, it's not difficult to concentrate on the lesbian-antics past and the many lesbian visitors present rather than the NT tea-towel image.

Most of the buildings are not open to the public: there is access to Vita's tower and to one room at ground-floor level. But this isn't a drawback – the gardens are far more interesting and pleasant. A study in carefully orchestrated wildness, modelled on the work of Gertrude Jekyll, these can get very busy, especially the famous white garden and herb garden, so a timed entrance system is in operation in an attempt to preserve their intimacy. It's not hard, though, to get away from the crowd: you can wander through the nuttery, lined with cob trees, walk down to the lake and lie down by the bullrushes. Even within the main garden area there are plenty of quiet, unexpected spaces, little grottos helpfully equipped with benches.

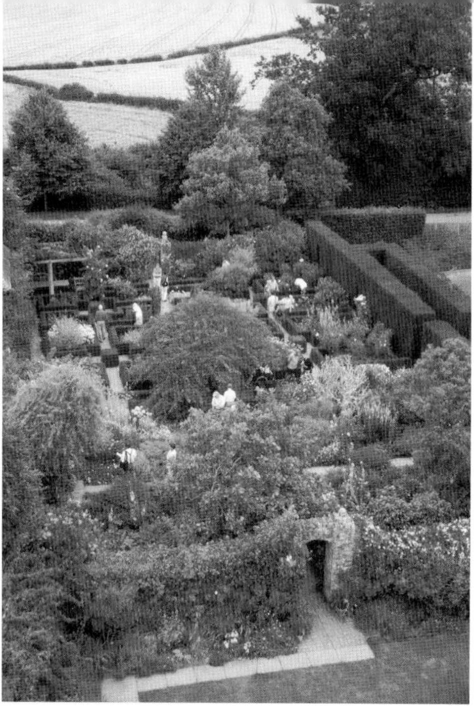

Sissinghurst Castle Gardens

Food can be a problem unless you eat to a NT timetable, which means lunch between 12.00 and 14.00 and cake only in the afternoon. Taking a picnic is a much better option. There's the usual shop selling NT ephemera and gardening books and also a 'farm shop' selling plants and such 'country fare' as mustards, flavoured oils, jams and biscuits.

A couple of minutes walk from the gardens is Sissinghurst Castle Farm, which offers bed and breakfast if you want to complete the experience (from £24 per person per night, April to October, call 01580 712885). And don't forget to take your jodphurs.

ADDRESS Sissinghurst House and Gardens, Sissinghurst, Kent (01580 715330)
OPEN 1 April to 15 October: Tuesday to Friday, 13.00–18.30; Saturday, Sunday and Good Friday, 10.00–17.30
ACCESS £6/free to NT members
ROAD about 1½ hours from London; M20/A20 to Maidstone, then A229

index

Index

Index

Index

PICTURES by Heike Löwenstein except:
page 5.41, Astrid Weiske
pages 7.3, 7.5, Keith Collie
page 7.19, National Portrait Gallery
page 7.21, Andrew Putler, National Portrait Gallery
page 9.23, Maria Satur

also available from ellipsis

London Walking
A Handbook for Survival

More than you could have imagined you needed to know to walk London, with vital advice to consider before you cross a road, *London Walking* is both practical guide and pointer to new possibilities.

The book includes useful discourse on subjects such as 'What is traffic?', how to recognise the kerb, and walking inside buildings; historical background on the Tufty Club and how to walk to escape the plague; more than 70 unhelpful illustrations; and an exercise in how far you can walk in a day following the sun. Armed with these appropriate strategies and techniques, it becomes possible to experience the city at its haptic, hectic best.

London Walking is a handbook for survival. Hard fact lies alongside personal commentary. Don't set foot on the pavement without it.

ISBN 1 84166 056 6
PRICE UK £10.00 US $15.00 (paperback)

Simon Pope

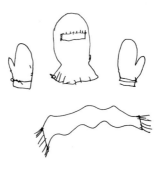

Lost mittens:

Nr. 1   Nr. 2   Nr. 3   Nr. 4

Beautiful Twisted Night

'Prostitutes, hustlers, porn stars, strippers, gangsters, pimps, domina-trixes, trans-sexuals, madams, subculture celebrities, superstars and even Satan worshippers' dance in and out of Marc Almond's 'beautiful twisted night'. Here, in a collection of his poetry, prose and lyrics of the last 20 years, is the city as a 'playground of fantasy and desire.'

Beautiful Twisted Night is a hard and loving look at the city streets, the red-light districts, the clubs and bars, the gay cultures and subcultures. It chronicles the dreams and disappointments of the city's inhabitants from the recognisable – Saint Judy – to the anonymous 'flotsam, jetsam, bottom-of-the-bin angels' – Exotica Rose, Jamie Dream, Champagne – from the bordello to the high-rise. Each of Marc Almond's albums is represented in the collection, and illustrations include drawings by Pierre et Giles as well as photographs from the author's personal collection.

ISBN 1 84166 023 X
PRICE UK £12.00 US $18.00 (paperback)

Marc Almond